Ransom Notes

Moments of Reflection, Courage,
Engagement, Worship, and Humor

KATHRYN ANN RANSOM

WESTBOW
PRESS®
A DIVISION OF THOMAS NELSON
& ZONDERVAN

Unless otherwise noted, Scripture quotations are taken from The Holy Bible, New International Version®, NIV® Copyright © 1973, 1978, 1984, 2011 by Biblica, Inc.® Used by permission. All rights reserved worldwide.

Scripture marked KJV taken from the King James Version of the Bible.

Scripture taken from The Message. Copyright © 1993, 1994, 1995, 1996, 2000, 2001, 2002. Used by permission of NavPress Publishing Group.

Scripture marked RSV taken from the Revised Standard Version of the Bible, copyright © 1946, 1952, and 1971 the Division of Christian Education of the National Council of the Churches of Christ in the United States of America. Used by permission. All rights reserved.

WestBow Press books may be ordered through booksellers or by contacting:

WestBow Press
A Division of Thomas Nelson & Zondervan
1663 Liberty Drive
Bloomington, IN 47403
www.westbowpress.com
1 (866) 928-1240

ISBN: 978-1-9736-5597-8 (sc)
ISBN: 978-1-9736-5598-5 (hc)
ISBN: 978-1-9736-5596-1 (e)

Library of Congress Control Number: 2019902802

Print information available on the last page.

WestBow Press rev. date: 03/29/2019

To my mother
Thankful for her guidance, modeling of a rich
Christian life, and constant inspiration.

Preface

RANSOM NOTES BEGAN SEVERAL years ago as the author worked with a class of adults at South Side Christian Church in Springfield, Illinois. In the beginning, the comments were brief and shared space on a single sheet of paper with a few jokes, announcements, and slogans. Gradually, as she gained confidence, the essay would fill one side of the sheet. The focus shifted a bit.

Joining the ranks of mature adulthood, and interacting with them each week, her perspective of this stage of life evolved. Despite what many seemed to believe, folk over fifty still had energy, useful skills, and experience worthy of sharing with others. Many were retired with time available to use in God's service. Rocking in a chair or simply tending pansies and petunias in the yard filled only a small need. All humans need focus, meaningful opportunities for engagement, and challenges to produce smiling days. Even our brains need feeding with thought-provoking reminders and reflection.

In addition, she observed that frequently her contemporaries were lonely or confined to home, either willingly or because of a variety of disabilities. Some of these adults yearned for the good old days when friendship and serving were a part of their lives. Connections and outreach were difficult goals.

Thus, the essays became a tiny gem of an idea. Could she, through sharing bits of wit, wisdom, and challenge, encourage folks to get up and step out? Her goal was to encourage others to get out of their chairs, enter their community, and become living examples of God's love for others. The essays share stories of humans doing exciting things for the Kingdom. Stories and challenges are based on examples of God's people growing and goofing throughout the ages. All are designed to help provide meaning to the lives of everyday folks while perhaps having just a bit of fun or a tiny chuckle, often at her expense, as she shared her own moments of weakness, discouragement, and forgetfulness.

Her goal today is that you, the reader, may find some challenge or example that strikes your heart to move forward in your Christian life in service for others. As you interact with the text, she hopes you will experience a gleam in your eye, spirit in your step, and meaningful moments as you tumble into bed at night.

Now, friends, go forth and share the Jesus that loves each of us.

Acknowledgments

WHAT A JOY TO share some thoughts and passions of my life in this collection of essays. None of this would have been possible, however, without the encouragement of many friends from coast to coast. I thank them for gently nudging me to step out on faith, grab my computer, and give it a go.

I am deeply thankful for the specific input, talent, and energy of several friends as we plodded through the creation. Terry Black's artistic talents helped with some of the graphics and text. Allan Shears's assistance with upgrading many of the photos was essential to the project. Kerma Yotter shared her wisdom as we worked on technical aspects of the book, and Lynn Poling provided thoughtful input. Without a doubt, however, nothing would have been possible without the editing talent of Rosanne Elder. I humbly thank each of them.

Staff assistance at WestBow Press, especially that of Venus Gamboa, helped light my path, as together we tackled the novice's publishing inexperience. Previous efforts at written communication had been limited to single-page copy. The reality of converting a simple essay into a collection of one hundred-plus pieces, designed to be printed in a book, was initially overwhelming. At times, it seemed we took two steps forward and one backwards. Giving up entered my mind. Then, a call or email from the staff yanked me out of my depression, and on we plodded. Thanks to the gang at WestBow, including my initial contact with the company, Eric Schroeder, whose guidance and encouragement from the very first phone contact lighted my path.

I am so blessed to be surrounded by a host of Christian friends. May their talents and caring spirit show through the words that follow. I also pray that readers will see the love of Christ reflected in the words and be drawn closer to the One who loves each of us. In addition, I hope that following reflection and prayer, you will be motivated to even greater service for the Kingdom.

Special Note

All Scripture quotations, unless otherwise indicated, are taken from the Holy Bible, New International Version, Copyright 1973, 1978, 1984 by International Bible Society.

Used by permission of Zondervan Bible Publishing.

Other translations used are Revised Standard Version (RSV), King James Version (KJV), and The Message.

Contents

Is Your Life a Wreck? If Yes, So What?

God restores, rebuilds, renews, and uses.
He has a plan for you.
What a mess!
Crumpled bumpers; rusted roof; missing tires;
sagging door; windows smashed; car is a disaster.
Not even spring flowers can overcome the misery described.

TURN ON YOUR IMAGINATION switch. Visualize the scene of an ancient auto described above. Project your thoughts into the mind of the driver who might have just crashed his cherished driving machine into a fence. Rain splashes down. Strangers encircle his vehicle. Maybe the individual is late for a meeting. His thoughts wander to future repair costs versus trashing the car and returning to his old horse and buggy. This is definitely not the best day of his life.

Sometimes, our lives resemble this miserable, drippy, foggy, crumpled, imaginary scene. Maybe even you, the reader, remember a time in your life when you were desperately in need of an "auto repair" shop. If that is true, where can you locate a viable model? Let's take a peek at some great Bible examples.

Think about Jonah. Distraught with the job God wanted him to do, he decided to turn tail and run to Tarshish. Off to the sea, but oh, what troubles. A giant storm battered the ship until even the professional sailors were terrified. Jonah volunteered to be thrown overboard, admitting that he was running away from God. Scared, wet, and worried—what happened? Swallowed, into the mouth of a large fish. For three days, Jonah curled up inside a stinking water creature and prayed (Jonah 1 and 2). Talk about disaster.

And then God took over again. Spit up onto the shore, Jonah probably washed himself off, grabbed a bite to eat, and set off on a three-day walk to Nineveh to preach. He finally got around to obeying God's orders. The people listened to this humble servant, repented, and trusted God (Matthew 12:41). A city was saved because of the changed life of a disobedient servant. Hmmm.

Or what about Paul? Disaster filled his life multiple times. Beaten with rods three times, whipped with thirty-nine lashes five times, bitten by poisonous vipers, shipwrecked, and stoned and left for dead: a tough list of disasters. He even was given a thorn in the flesh, which caused a great burden (2 Corinthians 12:7). Yet despite these disasters, the Lord told him, "My grace is sufficient for you, for my power is made perfect in weakness" (2 Corinthians 12:9). Paul was a leader, a defender of the faith, an encourager for the churches, and even at times a prod to move the followers forward. People probably related to Paul partially because of his calamities. God took his wrecked life, applied quick first-aid, and sent him back on the road to witness and serve.

And then there is John. As the churches grew and the Christians became more influential, the government leaders took action. Christians were treated with disrespect, as they were prohibited from getting jobs or buying goods in the markets. Sometimes even severe persecution resulted. John was no exception. As he reached the midnight of his life, we find him imprisoned on the island of Patmos. His life had crashed. Did "Poor me!" fill his thoughts? Giving up was not in his DNA. No way. Out of this disaster, John grabbed his quill and recorded the vision God provided.

Today, we each can share the wonderful hope recorded by John in the book of Revelation. God took that battered body and rebuilt a leader.

If God made over Jonah, Paul, and John, He can do the same with you, regardless of your wrecked life. You may be experiencing a disaster of tired muscles, hurting heart, broken relationship, job loss, death of a child, confinement to your home, diminishing financial resources, pain beyond description, or just a lack of energy. Wise up. He still needs you. No shutting down. Pray. Ask for guidance for a new way of service. Keep your eyes open to recognize the new path. Rebuild and restore your heart and connections with God.

**Then hop on your motor scooter. Restart
your engine and take off.
Be a bright and shining light for the King.**

Life inside a Tortoise Shell

PICTURED IS A UNIQUE drawing of a tortoise—well, really just half of that reptile, drawn by Terry Black. The shell is normally crammed with a collection of internal organs: lungs, thyroid, spleen, gallbladder, and liver, among others. The shell itself includes the turtle's spinal cord and rib cage. Interestingly also, the tortoise is attached to the shell and may not crawl away from it as other shell creatures often do. He just retracts his head and legs in and out, and the house follows along. The spine is extremely flexible and curls around among the organs within the tortoise skeleton. Incredible.

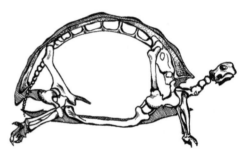

(drawing by T. BlacK)

This picture depicts emptiness, hollowness, or a void. The sketch clearly identifies the tortoise, but I immediately felt sad. Why? All that remains is the shell. One is left with a feeling of walking death. Even the skeleton face gives the impression of discouragement or defeat. Hope is gone. Life is over.

Sometimes, people also feel empty and defeated. Life seems grim and troubles insurmountable. Pain, worries, disappointments, or grief often reduce humans to a sense of walking death. The tortoise is going absolutely nowhere in this condition. He is done. That can happen to people too. The challenge for each of us, however, is to find ways that we can avoid becoming the walking dead.

When we become extremely discouraged, bitter, worn out, or defeated, we, too, may figuratively withdraw within ourselves. We shut out acts of kindness. Darkness and hate become companions as we huddle within our shells. Wrinkles, frowns, grumpiness, and anger fill our lives. Joy and thanksgiving for the gift of salvation, family, or friendship are absent from our thoughts. Words of rejoicing and celebration are history. We have died in our relationship with Christ and God. Result: we are miserable.

In Psalm 22:1–2, we hear David shouting out, "My God, my God, why have you forsaken me? Why are you so far from saving me, so far from the words of my groaning? O my God, I cry out by day, but you do not answer, by night, and am not silent." Christ on the cross uttered this prophetic message by David (Mark 15:34). For the moment, Christ experienced His human side, acknowledging the abandonment of God in order to die as the ultimate sacrifice for our sins. At that moment, He literally died. His spirit left Him (Matthew 27:50). The shell of His body remained on the cross.

We rejoice and hope today because of that lonely action on the cross. Why can we rejoice? Jesus set the example. Within days of His death, He was up and rejoicing with His followers. His mere presence encouraged these mourning, despondent leaders. He brought renewed vigor and spring to their step. Off they zipped to proclaim the gospel. The world was turned upside down because of their faith and hope.

David followed up his message of discouragement recorded in Psalm 22 with the glorious words of the Twenty-Third Psalm. The Lord is my shepherd, and He will take care of me through rough waters, troubled days, and even death. Reread his words if you, too, are experiencing an empty heart and soul. You are not alone. Take a moment also to read Psalm 51, especially beginning with verse seven.

> "Cleanse me with hyssop, and I will be clean; wash me, and I will be whiter than snow. Let me hear joy and gladness; let the bones you have crushed rejoice.… Create in me a pure heart, Oh God and renew a steadfast spirit within me" (Psalm 51:7–11).

Or as the modern translation in The Message states,

> "Soak me in your laundry and I'll come out clean. Scrub me and I'll have a snow-white life. Tune me in

to foot-tapping songs, set these once-broken bones to dancing. Don't look too close for blemishes. Give me a clean bill of health.... Don't throw me out with the trash, or fail to breathe holiness in me" (Psalm 51:7–11).

Seek out joy. Smile as you reach out to others experiencing dark days. Fill that empty shell of loneliness and sorrow with singing His praises. Extend your neck from your shell, and care for others. As we concentrate on praising God and caring for those in darkness, our own soul and spirit will be renewed.

Take a chance. Fill your empty heart with action on behalf of hurting neighbors. You will find you are suddenly filled with joy—even if a few tears remain.

"You Don't Throw Something Out Just Because It Has a Wrinkle"

ABOUT TWO YEARS AGO, I visited a former college roommate who lived on a dairy farm in Ohio. While chatting and cooking in the kitchen, I noticed that the light and fan in her microwave were not working. After I commented about the inoperative elements, she replied, "You don't throw something out just because it has a wrinkle." Considering that Pat had serious health issues at the time, the statement was even more thought provoking. Actually, I was intrigued by the implications of the comment.

Have we become a throwaway generation? Repair and recover require time and money. It seems like folks just toss out the clock that does not tick-tock and buy a new-generation creation. Have repair people been replaced with salespeople? Are our citizens over sixty-five becoming insurance risks instead of mentors to the young? Why are seniors often relegated to the back burner, when leadership, engagement, or innovation are needed? These and other scenarios twirled around in my head as I paid my last visit to a lifelong friend that day.

I was reminded again of Pat's quote this week as I laughed my way through the movie *Going in Style* with Morgan Freeman, Alan Arkin, and Michael Caine. These three retired steelworkers demonstrated just the opposite philosophy as they nimbly planned ways to recover money lost from their retirement funds through negative decisions by the bank. Although I do not condone their ultimate actions, I compliment their creativity, energy, and love of excitement, even though senior citizens. Visions of seventy-plus folks slumped in wheelchairs lining the halls of care centers haunt me. Life needs to be lived to the end with fullness and spirit. Of course, scaling mountains or climbing ladders to clean out the gutters may need younger bodies. Aching muscles greeted me following an afternoon of bagging leaves, but the leaves were ready to be thrown away—not me, the senior, wrinkled Kathy. There is still life ready for living at eighty-plus.

What does the Lord have to say about this "wrinkle, throwaway, dropout" philosophy of the twenty-first century? As one author put it, God had miraculous ways to use "ripened" saints. Seventy-five-year-old Abraham heard God's call to leave his homeland and start a new nation (Genesis 12:1–5). At one hundred, he and Sarah became parents of a son, Isaac (Genesis 21:1–7). You think you have it tough?

Think about Moses, another late-bloomer. When Moses was in his eighties, God captured his attention and sent him back to Egypt to encounter Pharaoh with an extremely unpopular request: "Let my people go." Tell Pharaoh, "My God wants you to give these folks, who have been your slaves for forty years, permission to leave." Granted, Moses trembled when God issued this order, but at least he had his hearing aid turned up, and off he went to fulfill the Lord's request (Acts 7:20–37). You certainly couldn't keep this old guy down in a rocker. Then imagine courage and strength required to leave his comfortable neighborhood, assemble a group of followers, and enter the desert area filled with dangers. He had to feed, clothe, and govern this group. He didn't even have a Humvee in which to ride or a handy McDonalds around every palm tree for a quick food fix. Praises to the old guys.

Isaiah shared God's promise for each of us today: "Even to our old age and gray hairs I am he, I am he who will sustain you. I have made you and I will carry you; I will sustain you and rescue you" (Isaiah 46:4). So the promise of God is He will always be with us, even to the years of our gray hair. (I suppose that also includes folks who conceal the gray.) God does not say quit. His command is, go into all the world and preach (serve, share, work, tell the story) until the end—not when the candles on the cake number sixty, seventy-two, or ninety-three.

Paul wrote letters of encouragement even while in prison. Jesus prayed to His Father even while hanging on the cross. What are you doing today for the Kingdom? No grumbling. No excuses. He is there. Reach out and take His hand in service and in prayer. Ignore the wrinkles and aches. Keep on keeping on.

Someone who is hurting, crying, or angry needs your love now.
No throwaways allowed today.
Shake off those inhibitions and aches.
Get Going.

Don't Teach the Bible

How Crazy Is That? How Heretical?
What in the World Is the Writer Suggesting?

HAS KATHY GONE WILD, suggesting we study the trendy L.L. Bean catalog rather than the Ten Commandments? Does the author want us to zip over to the library and grab copies of the *Girl Scout Handbook* for our bedtime study instead of reading from Mark or 1 Timothy? If that is true, why even come to church? She must be nuts.

I will leave it to the reader's judgement as to the mental condition of this scribe. I, too, was a bit shocked, however, when I read in a bulletin published by Plain Truth Ministries, a rather interesting statement. "Studies of sermon topics and titles reveal that the vast majority of messages given within the churches of Christendom, perhaps up to 80%, are centered on the needs and desires of human beings, rather than on Jesus Christ." Yes, 80 percent.

The real goal of reading and studying the authentic gospel of Christ is to teach Christ. The purpose of a Christ-centered lesson (or sermon) is not to teach the Bible but to "preach Christ crucified" (1 Corinthians 1:23). Of course, the Bible is all about Jesus Christ. He is the divine author and also the theme for our message. The goal, however, is to know Christ. But we seem to get sidetracked.

What happens too frequently in classes, articles, or sermons with our content? Do we discuss and study, but miss the main point, that all our life should be Christ centered? Even though we call ourselves "Bible-believing Christians" or "students of the Word," what is the focus of too many lessons? Have we shoved Christ out of the center of our teaching and taken comfortable detours? Let's think about what is really happening too frequently in our Bible classes and study groups There are at least three areas of concern.

1) The focus of our message often dwells on laws, rules, and morals. We encourage our listeners to focus on "thou shalt nots"—not kill, steal, commit adultery, or beat your children. The challenge often is to help more, care more, and increase our humility and patience. There is nothing wrong, of course, with being helpful, kind, meek, or tenderhearted. The scriptures even admonish us and challenge us to wrap ourselves in these Corinthian characteristics. But our life is more than longsuffering, gentleness, being kind to our parents, or avoiding murdering a colleague. Folks with no Christian affiliation practice that kind of life. Our life is to be Christlike. We died to self. We were raised again in His image. The focus is to let Christ live and dwell inside each of us. Our body is the "temple of God."

A Christian doesn't refrain from gossip just because it is a nasty habit, but because Christ is in us and gossip would not be a part of His being. He is truth, and He lives within us. Only being good for goodness sake is no better than those outside of Christ's love who exhibit truthfulness. Even non-followers of Christ generally teach their kiddos to not kick the neighbor in the shins but to smile and share pleasant conversation. The pursuit of being good can become just a legalistic chase without Christ as our center being. Along with being a good neighbor, let's excite our students with the hard truths of the scripture.

2) Too often, our message appears to present Christ as if He were a new, revised version of Moses: a lawgiver. We share the new version of the old law. For example, Moses shared God's law: "Thou shall not murder" (Exodus 20:13). Jesus said, "But I tell you that anyone who is angry with his brother ... will be subject to the judgement" (Matthew 5:22). This assumes that our relationship with God is based on laws. Instead, under the new covenant with God, laws are not the center of our relationship, but Jesus is the center—resulting in *love* as the key word versus laws.

3) How-to books, sermons, and lessons are a subtle departure from Christ as the center of our faith.

- how to be a Christian parent
- how to be a Christian in the workplace
- how to pray
- how to study the Bible
- how to manage your money as a Christian
- what to say at a time of death

Of course, these themes are important and often helpful with our daily life, but they are not a replacement for Christ. If we have Christ as the center post, we will want to talk with Him. Prayer will come naturally. As Christ dwells within us, putting others first, avoiding arguments, or being helpful will again direct our workplace actions. How-to books on office behavior will be unnecessary. Christ will be shining through you. Without Jesus, studying these how-to topics is just trying to pull yourself up by your own bootstraps.

The Kingdom of heaven is not focused on good deeds. We cannot work our way into heaven. Jesus reveals a new way of acting—a changed "you." He is central to our lives. We need daily fellowship. In 1 John 1:1–4, we are instructed to have fellowship with this Jesus to make our joy and life complete. This fellowship is more than just conversation, cups of coffee, and muffins before class. It is more than just meeting in a building on Sunday with other Christians who believe like we do. The unifying element is not a church name, but our faith in Jesus.

Preach Christ. Preach Christ daily in your life. Yes.
Do study the Bible, but focus on Christ and what
He said and did as He lived here on earth.
Not just a purpose-driven life, but a Christ-
centered life that is purpose driven.

("Christianity without the Religion," Plain
Truth Ministries, November 2, 2015.)

Did You Know a Group of Sea Turtles Is Called a Bale?

THIS LINE CAUGHT MY attention in an ad for Geico. Curiosity provoked me to Google the names of other groups of animals. The most amazing finding was how many of those group names could easily refer to Christians. I found it surprising. See what you think.

Quickly start guessing what connections popped into my head as I perused the list. Perhaps other ideas will cause your brain to quiver and shake with ideas. If yes, wonderful. Stimulation of the brain keeps us young.

- **Beavers and sardines: a family.** "God said, 'I will dwell in them and walk among them;... And I will be a Father to you, and you shall be sons and daughters to Me" (2 Corinthians 6:14–18). We are part of a family—the family of God. Let's join our beaver and sardine friends in celebration of all that family means, including love, cooperation, and support.

- **Bats and grasshoppers: a cloud.** "Therefore, since we are surrounded by such a great cloud of witnesses, let us throw off everything that hinders and the sin that so easily entangles. Let us run with perseverance the race marked out for us" (Hebrews 12:1). It is not just teachers who have eyes in the back of their heads. Someone is watching you right now. Check on yourself. Will you be happy to have our Father and a cloud of witnesses hearing and seeing what you are thinking or doing at the moment? Hopefully, the Lord is smiling at what He is viewing, but occasionally, there could be a tear in His eye.

- **Alligator: a congregation.** In Greek, the word *ekklesia* became the term for the Christian congregation, the church. We are a people called by God to receive salvation through Jesus Christ. Christians are people special to God. I am afraid, however, that followers often act more like alligators, devouring Christian brethren with angry words and actions rather than building loving relationships.

- **Caterpillars and frogs: an army.** Ephesians 6:10–18 describes a Christian's armor including breastplate, helmet, sandals, and shield, so we must be part of an army. We are to put on our armor of righteousness, peace, and faith, moving forward with prayer. Perhaps it takes an army of caterpillars or frogs to model our military connections.

- **Zebras: a zeal.** "Never be lacking in zeal, but keep your spiritual fervor, serving the Lord" (Romans 12:11). Just as a group of zebras is a zeal, so a group of individual Christians must exemplify a zealous life. Paul reminds the Romans that we are to be devoted to one another, keeping up our spiritual fervor, serving the Lord with eagerness. Are you zealous, or are you apathetic? Zebras sleep standing up—ready for action and defense. We, too, must stand tall, ready for action.

- **Lions: a pride.** Who is more proud than a lion, king of the jungle? Yet look at what Solomon states: "Pride goes before destruction, a haughty spirit before a fall" (Proverbs 16:18). We had better snuff out our lion characteristics and not think of ourselves more highly than we ought. Paul also talks about pride in Galatians 6:1–4, reminding us not to compare ourselves to others. Incidentally, many of us find that a challenge. Both good and destructive comparisons are made daily between ourselves and others and even between children and their friends. Be cautious that you do not deceive yourself, my lion friends.

Remember: A group of Christ followers is called Christians. We wear His name. Make Him proud.

Open Your Eyes; Run with the Lord

"In the beginning God created the heavens and the earth" (Genesis 1:1).
"The heavens declare the glory of God; the skies
proclaim the work of his hands" (Psalm 19:1).
"The mountains and hills will burst into song before you, and
all the trees of the field will clap their hands" (Isaiah 55:12).
"How beautiful on the mountains are the feet of those who brings good
news, who proclaim peace, who bring good tidings, who proclaim
salvation, who say to Zion, 'Your God reigns!'" (Isaiah 52:7).

IT HAS BEEN MY privilege to travel extensively throughout God's world
during my lifetime. Recently, we enjoyed a trip to the southern part of
Africa. Encountering the wildlife up close and personally continues to be
a joy. Catching the eye of an elephant in the camera lens thrills my heart.

Watching a mama lion protect her twin cubs from invading jeeps loaded with awestruck visitors is breathtaking. The wildlife, indeed, "declare the glory of God" (Psalm 19:1).

Following our return, I received an email from Dr. Paul Boatman, a friend in Lincoln, Illinois. He gave permission to share one of his memories while visiting in Masai Mara Reserve, Kenya:

> We spent the night in a tented camp in Masai Mara, and I arranged to have security in the morning for my daily run. At 6 a.m. I unzipped the tent and found a Masai Warrior with a spear. His job was to keep me safe as I was running through some of the same area where the previous afternoon we saw a pride of lions dismembering and eating a zebra. But he seemed to misunderstand his role. He apparently thought he was to set a Kenyan runner pace. In light of the proximity of lions, I was highly motivated to attempt to keep up, but whenever I got within twenty meters, he sprinted ahead. I think it was my fastest run ever.
>
> The following morning we were with missionaries up on the escarpment. I went running alone and encountered a group of giraffes who watched me from as close as ten meters. I was also startled by a family of topis [large antelopes]. I had to halt my run while a single-file gang of baboons marched across the trail upon which I was running.
>
> I am invigorated by encounters with God's creation.

We, too, had guards with guns as we returned to our huts at night. Believe me, though, I never went running—running period—let alone with a Masai warrior. Two ideas, however, raced through my gray head as I read Paul's commentary.

First, as we run along the path of life crowded with dangers, challenges, worries, and even warriors, we have our Masai guard by our side. Psalm 121 describes this protection plan: "He won't let you stumble.... Israel's Guardian will never doze or sleep. God's your Guardian, right at your side to protect you.… God guards you from every evil, he guards your very life" (Psalm 121 The Message). We do, however, have to keep running—keep on keeping up. Paul kept his eye on his guardian. What about you? Remember, God never slumbers or sleeps.

And then Boatman's last sentence: "I am invigorated by encounters with God's creation." How can we not bow before that statement? My friends, look out the window, stare at the stars, cuddle the kitty, watch the eagle soar, admire your grandchild. God made them.

While recognizing God's creative genius, run—run like the wind. Escape the dark moments in your head. Abandon those pity parties. Dash out to lend a hand to a needy neighbor. Leap with eagerness at each opportunity to sing praises to our Savior. Mentally dart around, searching for someone who is hurting; exhort and lend a smile or word of encouragement. We can't outrun God, but we can attempt to keep up.

Open your eyes; Run with the Lord.

God's Plan for You

HAVE YOU EXPERIENCED THE frustration of not knowing what to do with your life? Have you encountered life's road map as blank or confusing? Did you feel the chill of being in a dark tunnel minus a light guiding your steps? Were *fear, frustration, helplessness, uncertainty, or discouragement* words that popped into your brain? This writer has experienced that tunnel.

High school days were rapidly coming to an end in 1953. What was I going to do with my life? Where would I go to college? What did the Lord want me to do? With some nudging and help from our minister, my mother dropped me off at Ozark Christian College. It was a wonderful experience, but this sense of a need for a real plan for my life lingered. Although I loved my classes and friends, a clear vision of a job escaped me. After sleepless nights, prayer, and conversation with my parents, I changed schools and off to teachers' college I went, but I still had the nagging worry over what was the plan for my life. Where would the Lord lead me? Did He even need me? Dark, sad, discouraging thoughts crowded my waking moments.

Recently my attention was drawn to a passage from Jeremiah, which I needed sixty-five-plus years ago: "'When seventy years are completed for Babylon, I will come to you and fulfill my gracious promise to bring you back to this place. For I know the plans I have for you,' declares the Lord, 'plans to prosper you and not to harm you, plans to give you hope and a future. Then you will call on me and come and pray to me, and I will listen to you. You will seek me and find me when you seek me with all your heart. I will be found by you,' declares the Lord, 'and will bring you back from captivity. I will gather you from all the nations and places where I have banished you,' declares the Lord, 'and will bring you back to the place from which I carried you into exile'" (Jeremiah 29:10–14).

What message did God have Jeremiah relay to the elders and captives in Babylon? Be prepared for a long visit in this foreign land. Then the surprising comment: settle down. Build houses. Plant beans and squash. Marry and raise a family in spite of the unknown. Be faithful and don't listen to false voices that deceive you. I did not send them.

Why in the world would God tell these Jerusalem exiles that? My mind would be frantically trying to create an avenue of escape. Can we assemble a secret team to take Nebuchadnezzar out of play? How can I return my family to the Promised Land so we can fulfill God's plan? What in the world is God thinking, leaving us captive in this heathen country? Why would He allow false prophets to try to deceive us? Why God?

Let's look closely at God's words as He shares four action statements:"

- I will keep my promise.
- I have a plan for you; I want to give you a future and hope.
- I hear you when you pray, but you must pray for the welfare of Babylon so they will not harm you.
- I will bring you home, but wait seventy years. God does not always hurry in fulfilling His promises.

These Children of Israel did not know every detail of God's plan. They had an action plan, however: Live a normal life, even in uncertainty. Raise a family, eat, marry, and *pray*. Then trust. They had a choice, however. God did not make them pray or follow His plan. There would be light at the tunnel's end only if they followed His instructions.

So what about you? God will keep His promise to care for His own. He will be with you 24/7. Go forth and live a normal life, but sow the seeds of the gospel. You may find yourself in dreadful conditions with family, job, finances, or health, but keep praying. Keep living, loving, and worshipping. Don't be depressed and discouraged. God's folks in Babylon had no guarantee that life would be a bed of petunias. It could have been a bed of dandelions. They just knew that God would keep His promise. This is still a truth for us today.

God had a plan for me. I just didn't know what it was. He brought me to Springfield. He provided a church where I could serve and worship. He promises me life everlasting with Him someday. (No hurry, it seems.) In turn, I must pray, worship, serve, remain faithful, and trust, while simultaneously living a normal life.

You, too, have the same promise. There is hope, joy, and anticipation of singing praises with the heavenly chorus while standing around His throne someday.

Hang in there, friend of God.
Trust His plan for you and be a winner.

Is True Friendship Possible?

This, I realized suddenly, was friendship. You don't always agree, and you both may do things the other person wished you didn't, but it doesn't mean things come to a grinding halt. It doesn't mean you stop being friends. You got over it, and you moved on. Maybe most people worked this out earlier in life, but this was a revelation for me. In my family, there had been no room for error, at least not for me."
—Sara J. Henry

IN HER BOOK, A *Cold and Lonely Place*, Sara J. Henry shares her definition of friendship. As I read her words, my eyes paused, and my brain kicked in. "Hey, Kathy, that is a stunning thought. Wouldn't it be wonderful if I, Kathy, could always implement that concept?" A key to deep, meaningful relationships apparently involves learning to disagree in an agreeable manner. Is it possible to have conflict without combat? In today's world of polarization, can you develop lasting friendships with folks supporting extremely different ideas from yours? Some would say no. Christ would say that we must.

I scanned the words a number of times, remembering relationships with friends over my eighty-plus years. My very best friend for his entire life was my little brother, John (see picture). We traveled extensively as children, and growing up, he was actually the only friend I had until about sixth grade. He remained my confidant until his death. Did we always agree? Of course not. Do brothers and sisters ever always agree? Do cats and dogs never hiss and woof at each other? We learned to disagree, probably fight a bit, but then move on. You love and trust family, just as I trusted Little John. Even as an adult when visiting his family during my annual trip to Oklahoma, we would stay up very late one night just to share cares, joys, and requests for a listening ear. How I relished those few hours each Christmas. I've had many wonderful friends throughout my eighty-three years, but none ever gained the private, heartfelt, tell-it-all confidence that I experienced with him.

Well, yes. There is one other friend. Guess who? Who is the true friend who is closer than a brother? What better friend than Christ? "But God demonstrates his own love for us in this: While we were still sinners, Christ died for us" (Romans 5:8). This friend gave His life for me. But equally comforting is the promise we have when we are feeling hurt, lonely, frustrated, or discouraged. "The Lord himself goes before you and will be with you; he will never leave you nor forsake you. Do not be afraid; do not be discouraged" (Deuteronomy 31:8).

We acknowledge Christ's death on our behalf. We thank Him for His sacrifice when we participate in the Lord's Supper. We even sing "Jesus Loves Me" with fervor. But do we truly internalize that friendship and love? Do we just mouth a silent prayer as the Communion bread and juice are passed but then reflect on our anxieties and burdens? Have we forgotten what true friends do? He is our friend. Friends care. Friends cry with us. They listen and hold us in their arms and help us through troubled waters. That's just what Jesus did when those rugged fishermen Peter, James, and the others were scared to death during a windstorm on the lake. They cried out to the Master, their friend—and bless me. He rebuked the winds, and you know the rest of the story. Calm waters and smooth sailing resulted. But also remember, He asked those young disciples a tough question. It is the identical question each of us should ask ourselves when we are frightened and scared: "Where is your faith?" (Luke 8:25).

Back to our initial thought: can we remain friends and disagree, argue, question, or sometimes even hurt that individual? Of course, Henry is correct when she encourages us to have conflict without combat. But that is difficult for feisty folks like me. How about our relations with our friend Christ? Can we question Him? Will we sometimes get a bit angry with what is happening in our lives, blaming Him for our aching bodies, mounting bills, wayward grandchildren, yucky job, or deep despondency? Good friends will have moments of anger, disagreement, or frustration, but they ask forgiveness and move on.

So it is with our Christian life. When you are experiencing cat-and-dog behaviors, stop. Bend your knees. Open your heart, and cry out to Him in prayer. Shed a tear. Then make up.

**Give God a loving hug and renew your friendship.
He will never leave you or forsake you.**

Lessons from the Titanic

ONE AFTERNOON, I ATTENDED an organ concert at Westminster Presbyterian Church in Springfield. John Sherer was guest organist from Chicago. Although a church organist, one of his passions is the study of the tragic sinking of the "unsinkable" *Titanic* and music related to that event of April 1912. We were thrilled by his interpretations of music of 1912 as well as tunes actually played on this ship of steel. Of course, he included "Nearer My God to Thee."

Equally entertaining were the tales, facts, figures, and lessons learned from this ocean mishap. Costing $7.5 million ($400 million in 2017 dollars), the ship sailed from Southampton, England. Twenty-two hundred passengers plus crew and ship weighed seventy thousand tons as they departed. It was the largest ship ever made at that time. First-class suites cost $4,350 ($50,000 today). A third-class ticket cost $40. People in third class were unable, however, to go to the upper decks, thus making them more vulnerable for quick exit.

1601 DROWNED

A Terrible Calamity.

The Carpathia with the survivors of the Titanic wreck has arrived in New York. 1601 of the 2340 persons on board were drowned. Going full steam ahead in an effort to make a record trip, the vessel struck an iceberg and went down with a loss of life the like of which has not been known before. Charles M. Hayes, president of the Grand Trunk Railway, J. J. Astor, the millionaire and many other famous men were drowned, as with the band playing lively music the vessel sank in water two miles deep.

Barney after a 10

Frank son paid week.

Mr. N. of days in Tuesday.

Mr. and on Tuesda home in I

M. Mec ist, will b May 18th

Mr. J. spending guest of I Black.

Mr. Sk was on th days this desk agai

A new construction feature included sixteen watertight compartments designed to make the ship unsinkable if each was closed. Twenty lifeboats limited space to only 1,178 persons—immediately suggesting a problem for some of the 2,201 passengers. In addition, everyone was having such a glorious time at departure and crew so confident the vessel was unsinkable that a lifeboat drill was cancelled. Life jackets also were not available for all passengers.

Dr. Sherer shared other interesting facts. The steel for the boat was a type that, when frozen, could easily crack. Guess what happened when the ship arrived in icy water and hit an iceberg? In addition, during the testing of the ship, it was noted that the steering mechanism was not functioning correctly; the ship could not turn quickly or completely. This fact was ignored by the owners and not corrected. When the sirens were finally sounded, indicating the need to go quickly to the decks, don life jackets, and prepare for departure, the guests were having such a good time that they ignored the signals. The lookouts did not have binoculars, which reduced their ability to spot icebergs. Overconfidence, misplaced faith in construction design, and excessive celebrating contributed to the tragedy.

Sherer ended his comments with three lessons, which immediately made me think of applications for people today:

1. Don't be overconfident (even a ship made of steel with watertight compartments is not unsinkable).
2. Pay attention to details when someone is speaking (the turning mechanism should have been fixed; the sirens were ignored; the lifeboat drill was canceled).
3. Make the most of every day.

Now, think about this from the perspective of twenty-first-century folks and their relationship to Christ:

1. Don't be overconfident. Are there folks today who think their good deeds, contributions to charitable organizations, or visits to church for the annual Easter service will save them? They may even think they are unsinkable.
2. Pay attention to details when someone is speaking, especially if it is God. How many of your friends are not prepared with the lifejacket of Christ's saving blood? What can you do to help them listen and climb aboard the lifeboat? Are we too busy as followers

experiencing our own happy times that we ignore pleas from troubled folks for rescue?

3. Make the most of every day. We know not the day or hour when the Lord will return for His children. We know not when any of us might leave this world. We are charged to preach the gospel, to share love, to tell His story. Do that today—not tomorrow.

Are you helping launch lifeboats daily?
Remember:
Amateurs built the Ark; professionals built the *Titanic*.

He Lives! Yes, He Does

WE HAVE ALL READ "Dear [Somebody]" letters. Perhaps this one addressed to fictional advisor Amah may be of interest:

> Dear Amah, Our pastor said that Jesus swooned on the cross and then His disciples carried His body home, cared for him, restored Him to health, and sent Him on his way. Please help me. Signed, Curious

> PS. Amah, I think your name in Hebrew means "having the answer," so I know you will provide a reliable response. Thank you.

Amah responded,

> Dear Curious, Whip your pastor with a cat-o'-nine-tails thirty-nine times and slam a crown of thorns on his head. Nail his hands and feet to a cross and let him hang by his arms for six hours. Pierce his side with a spear, and put him in an airless tomb for thirty-six hours and see what happens.
>
> Sincerely, Amah.

What would you say if someone asked you if Christ rose from the dead? Would you say, "Yes, of course, He rose from the grave," or would you stumble and say, "Uh. Well, uh, they keep telling me that at church, but I don't really know"?

How do I know? Let's review a few important pieces of information. First, several hundred people witnessed His presence many times following the resurrection. From the women at the empty tomb (Matthew 28:5–7) to the fellows walking along the Emmaus Road, their stories ring in my ears. He was alive. They saw Him. They spoke to Him. They ran and told others about this miraculous reappearance. Over five hundred eyewitnesses, on at least eleven different occasions, over forty days recognized Jesus following the resurrection.

Second, history supports the resurrection. Following His resurrection, many were willing to give their lives for him. Ancient Bible scholars and historians, including Josephus, Pliny, and Tacitus, each believed and wrote about this miracle.

Some say His body was stolen that night. If the body of Jesus went missing during the night while in the tomb, the soldiers guarding would have been killed for neglect. Falling asleep on your guard duty job was not tolerated by the Romans. In addition, if the leadership had taken the body, when the followers of Christ claimed He had risen, they would have just brought out the stolen body for display.

The identity of Jesus was confirmed by Himself (John 14:6). God verified it (Mark 9:7). Both His followers and His enemies acknowledged the resurrection (Mark 8:27–30 and John 10:33). The historian Pliny in AD 111 also believed it to be true. And then—wonders of wonders—we have over seven hundred fulfilled prophecies from the OT predicting this event was to happen.

The death of Jesus was undisputed at the time by friend and foe. As the writer Amah said in reply to Dear Curious, He really died. After being flogged, beaten, hung on a cross, poked with a spear, and placed in a tomb for three days—of course, he died. The guards stood by. The Roman seal was placed on the stone. Some say the tombstone would have needed twenty husky guys to roll it away. No one person could steal Jesus's body. Even the centurion and others guarding the tomb saw the earthquake and what took place and acknowledged, "Surely he was the Son of God!" (Matthew 27:54).

One of the most compelling reasons for belief in the bodily resurrection of Christ was the changed behavior of the disciples and other followers. These guys were willing to die for Him. The church in Jerusalem exploded in growth. Christians spread throughout the known world, telling the story. Lives were changed in spite of fear of persecution.

The resurrection was real. The resurrection enthroned Jesus as the Messiah. Because He rose from the dead, He guarantees our resurrection. If Christ had not conquered death, there would be no hope, no promise, no salvation.

The Resurrection does matter.
Hallelujah.

Chatty Kathy: Surprise Findings

According to a headline in *Condé Nast*
Traveler on February 6, 2016,
"Oregon Is the Fastest Speaking State in the U.S."

THE ARTICLE CONTINUED, "APPARENTLY, Oregon is full of Chatty Cathys. The Beaver State just made its debut as the fastest talking state in the nation, speaking six words in the time it takes the rest of us to spit out five words."

As I read, I thought, *Whoopee! They are talking about me.* I was born in Portland, Oregon, in 1935, which qualified me as a possible speedy talker. And then guess what nickname I received shortly after I arrived at my first teaching job in Springfield in 1958? "Chatty Kathy." Chatty Cathy dolls were in vogue. The staff at Iles School often referred to me by that popular name. I have n-o-o-o idea why I was given that nickname! I am certain, however, this must be an incredibly reliable study, since over four million phone calls were made during the survey.

If you are from the Upper Midwest, you are also probably part of this elite group of "fast talkers." You can guess where the slowest speech pattern is found—the South, especially those folks from Louisiana, Alabama, and the Carolinas. Mississippi came crawling in dead last. By the way, New Yorkers talk more than any other state, using sixty-two percent more words than residents of Iowa, where they speak the fewest words.

Now the reason for sharing this strange piece of research. What are we "saying" with all of those speedy words? Are we really just chatting about slippery streets, the price of Clorox, or the goofy next-door neighbor? Do we chatter mostly about our grandchild's latest cute saying? Are our mouths grumbling and irritating our friends and family? Do we sound like Grumpy Gus, Gossipy Gail, or Sappy Sis? But especially, are we reflecting God in our speech, or just mundane nonsense?

"Let your conversation (way of life) be always full of grace, seasoned with salt, so that you may know how to answer everyone" (Colossians 4:6). "With the tongue we praise our Lord and Father, and with it we curse human beings, who have been made in God's likeness. Out of the same mouth come praise and cursing. My brothers and sisters, this should not be" (James 3:9–10).

Of course we must visit with friends about everyday tasks, families, and even golf scores or politics. But immersed in that conversation let us Sing Forth Praises to the God of our Salvation. We must also dare to "Speak Up" when observing or hearing others sharing untruths or exhibiting prejudice. Watch for hurting folks and reach out with words of comfort and kindness. Expressing sorrow or sadness should fill our conversation when viewing inequity or cruelty. Whether we speak rapidly or with a southern drawl, let folks know we are Children of God.

One final reminder, however. Samuel the prophet said it so well as He was having a conversation with God. "Speak, Lord, for your servant is listening" (1 Samuel 3:1–10). The Chatty Kathys of our world often open mouth and out pops a flow of words. Samuel would suggest that engaging the brain prior to speaking is a valuable lesson. Listen! Then speak out on behalf of Christ. Jesus says it best as He visits with the twelve regarding John the Baptist.

"He who has ears, let him hear" (Matthew 11:15).
Dare to speak up, but graciously, not obstreperously.
Polite is still okay.

Good Intentions Lead to Embarrassment

THE PHONE RINGS, AND I answer politely, "Kathy speaking." A voice mumbles a bit, but I finally decide that the call is from the church with a need for food at next day's funeral dinner. Would I be willing to bring a salad? My mind mentally visualizes the calendar. Wednesday is early morning golf league. I'm torn. Helping out is a high priority for me, but golfing is relaxing. Could I manage to do both? Of course! Set the alarm for six o'clock, create a salad while gulping down my toast and coffee, swing by the church, drop off my creation, and then hustle on to golf for an eight o'clock tee-off.

Having made this creative timeline, I replied to the lady on the phone that yes, I would be delighted to deliver a salad for the luncheon the next day. We hang up. As evening approaches, I go to the kitchen, chop up the various ingredients for my salad, and arrange bowls so that things will go swiftly and smoothly in the morning.

Off to bed. Morning dawns, coffee cup in hand, I swiftly assemble the salad, put on golf shoes, and dash to the church, where I place the salad in the refrigerator, and scurry to the golf course.

Three hours later, golf game completed, I hop in the car and think, *Wouldn't it be nice if I dropped by the church to see if help is needed to serve the food?* As I arrive at the parking lot, a strange feeling begins to form in my mind. Where are the cars? The lot has only a couple vehicles.

Is this a tiny funeral or what? Entering the church, I immediately see a member of the staff and inquire about the funeral. The strangest look comes over her face. "Funeral? I don't believe we have a funeral today," she tells me.

What is the problem? I have the date in my calendar. Reality sets in as I slowly realize that I've made a mistake. I wander down to the kitchen, retrieve my salad, and return home thinking, how could I make such an error? We have salad for lunch, and I take a large portion to our neighbors and my hairdresser as I reported for my weekly beautification. He gobbles down my gift with glee and gracious comments. I continued to wonder, Where did I get mixed up? Yuk.

Jesus was also involved with a death, but instead of showing up early with His gift, He arrived after Lazarus, his friend, had been in the tomb four days. When He told His disciples they are returning to Bethany because our friend has fallen asleep, they misunderstand. Jesus had to clarify that Lazarus has died. Martha, sister of the deceased, greeted Jesus with almost a challenge in her voice: "Lord, if you had been here, my brother would not have died. And even now I know that whatever you ask from God, God will give you." It is hard to imagine Martha's tone of voice as she said those words: a blend of sorrow, disappointment, and yes, even faith.

Of course, we all know the ending of the story. Jesus assures her that her brother will rise again. Martha assumes He means at the time of the resurrection. Jesus has other ideas. They call Mary, the other sibling, to come see Jesus. She falls at His knees, mumbling, "If you had been here, my brother would not have died." Jesus, troubled at her weeping and sorrow, shares His human side. He weeps. They then go to the gravesite and remove the stone, in spite of the outcry that it will stink, and Jesus calls Lazarus forth. Rejoicing follows, and many believe. (Read John 11:1–45 RSV.) What a joyful ending to this funeral event.

Two scenarios centered around death, sadness, and celebration. One of us failed to listen carefully, wanted to be thoughtful, arrived early, but was embarrassed for her mistake. Kathy cared, prepared, but failed. Jesus listened, counseled His disciples, and then finally walked to Bethany to find the bereaving family had buried their loved one four days earlier. What did Jesus do when He met the family? He comforted, counseled, and cried with the guests. I, on the other hand, just munched down my salad. John tells us in verse 45 that many of the Jews who came to console the family believed in Jesus. What a wonderful ending.

What are the lessons for us?

- Good intentions alone, without careful planning and attention to details, may benefit no one.
- Honest, heartfelt sympathy, tears, and raw emotions may enable one to be a valid witness for the Kingdom.
- Helping hurting people is sometimes a stinking job. We often want to get rid of a problem. Jesus faced it and won followers.
- Doing nothing but sit on our patios will accomplish little. We just must try harder the next (or perhaps listen more carefully).

And now, the rest of the story: As I related the adventure to my housemate, we decided that the original phone call was really from her church. The salad was expected for another family's funeral gathering. Apparently, I had not listened well and assumed that the caller was from South Side Christian. I had quickly, but wrongly, accepted the opportunity to share. She called her church office and apologized for the missing salad. We wondered who may have been hungry that noon.

So, listen.
Be patient but leap forward to serve.
Celebrate the results.

A New Creation

Cream of Green Bean Stem Soup

THANKSGIVING IS HISTORY FOR this year. Twenty-four little pilgrims arrived at our home on Thursday. Four generations were represented from Ohio, Indiana, Illinois, New York, Florida, and Iowa. A joyful time of visiting, hugging, listening to stories, and walking down memory lane was experienced by all. What a time of celebration.

Family reunions, however, are preceded by hours of food preparation, shopping, consulting with others, and maybe a tad of housecleaning. My tasks were simple and required little skill: mashed potatoes and green beans. Yes, I was entrusted with snipping bean stems and peeling potatoes. Big deal.

As I finished chopping off the ends of three pounds of green beans, a mound of stems stared at me. I started to deposit them in the garbage and then—bingo—a crazy ideas flooded my brain. Could they be salvaged or recreated? At our house, we recycle many food items, but never green bean stems.

What about soup? We use asparagus ends for soup. Why not bean stems? Lunchtime was approaching, so I grabbed a skillet and started melting butter to sauté chopped onions, green pepper, parsley, and garlic. While the bean stems simmered, I created a white sauce. After draining the steamed bean ends, I popped them in the blender, smashing the stems. Into the pot of white sauce went the mushed-up bean stems, along with spices I found handy. Who knows what was in the Trinidad lemon garlic marinade, but it accompanied a little lemon pepper and salt into the pot. I considered some pork rub mix sitting there, but somehow that didn't excite my taste buds. Pouring this mix into a pair of soup bowls and topping each with croutons, we had a rather pleasant if insane soup.

Now I doubt that my recipe will make next year's *Betty Crocker Cookbook*. In fact, I doubt that this new creation will ever see the light of day again, but it caused me to think—to think about the great promise in Revelation: "Then I saw a new heaven and a new earth; for the first heaven and the first earth had passed away.... And I saw the holy city, new Jerusalem, coming down out of heaven from God, prepared as a bride adorned for her husband; and I heard a great voice from the throne saying, "Behold, the dwelling of God is with men. He will dwell with them and they shall be his people, and God himself will be with them; he will wipe away every tear from their eyes, and death shall be no more, neither shall there be mourning or crying or pain any more, for the former things have passed away.... Behold I make all things new" (Revelation 21:1–5 RSV).

My humble culinary skills created an edible product. We ate it. We did not starve. I was glad there were no guests sharing my soup. What a contrast with the vision John had of our new city, the New Jerusalem. God's creative skills surpass the skills of the most inventive, brilliant designer the world has ever known. I was eager to taste the creamy green bean mixture in my bowl, basically to see how terrible it might be. In contrast, I can hardly wait until the day arrives when we will be able to join our Lord in His heavenly creation. He has prepared heaven especially for His children—you and me.

In fact, it is so special; it is a wedding. No cream of green bean *stem* soup at a wedding for the bride of Christ, the church. For the thirsty, He will provide free drinks from the fountain of life (Revelation 21:6). This new holy city, Jerusalem, will come down from heaven, given to us from God. It will display the glory of God with radiance like a most-rare jewel, like a jasper. The city will be pure gold, clear as glass.

This new city needs no sun or moon to shine, for the glory of God is its light. Aren't you delighted that God is the creator of our new dwelling place and not some soup-creating human being?

As John sums up his vision, remember the final words of God: "Surely I am coming soon. Amen. Come, Lord Jesus" (Revelation 20:22 RSV). What a time of rejoicing that will be.

"And God Created the Heavens and the Earth"

And God said, "Let there be lights in the expanse of the sky to separate the day from the night, ... and let them be lights in the expanse of the sky to give light on the earth." And it was so. God made two great lights—the greater light to govern the day and the lesser light to govern the night.... And God saw that it was good.
(Genesis 1:14, 15, 18)

WHAT WONDERS TO BEHOLD. God's creation held the nation's attention for several hours on August 21, 2017. Millions of viewers from Salem, Oregon, to the East Coast donned their special glasses, tipped their heads skyward, and stared in awe. Families traveled miles to watch the spectacular alignment of the sun, moon, and our earth. Stadiums and fields were crowded with vans, tents, campfires, and folks from one to ninety-one. Highways were jammed. Trips that normally took three hours dragged into nightmares of seven or more. News media focused cameras on the sky and on the skywatchers, producing wonders of God in print and in cyberspace. Commentators and scientists rambled endlessly but seldom, if ever, gave any acknowledgement to Him who made this wondrous experience possible.

On that Monday, millions of folks looked up. Perhaps you, too, tilted your eyes skyward. But what were you thinking? Did your head just say, "Eyes, this is so beautiful? Aren't we glad we grabbed these special glasses and stopped to see the changes in our sky"? Or did your heart also remind you of the Creator, the designer who was so perfect in His construction that scientists could predict to the minute the location of this phenomenon? Hopefully as you stared in awe, your mind reminded you that God and His Son are the center of this universe.

We must remember this as we share future dramatic experiences with family and friends. Perhaps an analogy might work. The actual visual we experienced represents a cake, delicious and tasty. The recognition of the creator could remind us of the chef who baked the cake. Which is greater, the product (cake) or the designer and creator? Without the chef, there would be no dessert. Without God, no solar eclipse would occur.

In the beginning, God saw that His creation was "good" as he reflected on His handiwork. That day, many of us whispered or shouted out, "This is good." Let us also take a moment for a silent prayer:

"Thanks, God, for the beauty of your earth. We appreciate the stability of the rotation of these created elements. We can depend on your faithful support of the system. Also, God, help each of us to be more cognizant of what we can do to preserve and care for the gift of earth given for our temporary use. Amen."

**May His sun provide each of us with sufficient
energy to proclaim to the world
His message of love for each of His children.
Go forth and shine for our Lord.**

God Is Love (1 John 4:16)

How Do We Know?

"THIS IS HOW GOD showed his love among us: He sent his one and only Son into the world that we might live through him" (1 John 4:9).

Why Should Christians Love?

"We love, because he first loved us" (1 John 4:19).

Who Must We Love?

- "Love the Lord your God with all your heart, and with all your soul, and with all your might" (Matthew 22:37 RSV).
- "Husbands love your wives" (Colossians 3:19 RSV).
- "Love your neighbors" (Matthew 22:37–39 RSV).
- "Love one another with brotherly affection" (Romans 12:10; 1 John 3:11 RSV).
- "Love your enemies and pray for those who persecute you" (Matthew 5:44 RSV).
- "He who loves God should love his brother also" (1 John 4:21 RSV).

How Do We Love?

- Love is a decision. It does not happen automatically. You must be intentional.

  It can take courage to exhibit love to
  - an enemy, whether a competitor or citizen from a country with whom we are at war,
  - a spouse, parent, or friend who treats you with disrespect,
  - a neighbor who fails to rake their yard or ignores your pleas for help while stuck in the snow,
  - a clerk or coworker who is rude or mean-spirited,
  - a teen who lacks normal courtesy skills, even including saying "good morning" or "thanks," or
  - a fellow Christian with whom you share a difference of opinions.

- Love is genuine, but hate is evil (Romans 12:9).

  - Love keeps God's commandment (John 14:15).
  - Love with compassion, sympathy, mercifulness, tenderheartedness
  - Love is patient and kind, not jealous or boastful or rude. Love does not get exasperated.
  - Love does not insist on its own way; it is not irritable or resentful (1 Corinthians 13:5).
  - Love values the other person and acts for the benefit of others. Have you extended a helping hand today?
  - Love is often quiet, unobtrusive, behind the scenes—not a fireworks display.
  - Love is loving the unlovable: the lost, lonely, outcast, or gal from the other side of the tracks.

Check out your love actions. Are you loving others?
We are made to be loved and to love.

"Food Consumed at Church Functions Does Not Count toward Daily Caloric Intake, Nutritionists Confirm"

MY EYES JUST ABOUT jumped out of my head as I read this headline recently. The *Babylon Bee* (September 14, 2017) captured my attention with the following: "Confirming an age-old rumor among churchgoers, world-class nutritionists at the U. of Wisconsin-Madison's Food Research Institute announced that any and all food consumed on church grounds or at a church function is exempt from counting toward one's caloric intake for the day."

They continue, "We've done numerous exhaustive studies on this and can now say without a doubt that calories consumed at church simply are not absorbed by the body," UW Lead Nutritionist, Philip Reed, reported at a press event. "We have no scientific explanation for this at the moment—it seems to be some sort of miraculous event that takes place inside the body of a believer when he or she is consuming delicious baked goods in the house of God."

My initial thoughts were, "Wonder if I could just plan to eat all meals at church?" This would be the most wonderful news of my lifetime. (Well, yes, certainly information regarding Christ's saving power exceeds this news in awesomeness.) Luscious berry pies and warm cheesy dishes whenever I wanted, with no negative results—what an exciting thought. My brain wondered immediately, *How could that be true? But if Jesus could turn water into wine, why not turn a baked potato into a calorie-free snack?*

Well, I expect this was only an eye-teaser headline, and yes, it worked. I stopped and reacted. No further explanation was found, despite my searching the internet. For two weeks, I pondered periodically, "What could these researchers really mean?" Finally, the light bulb of my imagination conceived a connection: The Word of God is the Bread of Life (John 6:35). Reading the scriptures and studying what God has to say will not increase our calorie intake, but it will assist in drawing us closer to God.

Christ reminds us in John 6:25–59 that food obtained from study of the Bible is from heaven and gives life to this world. This knowledge endures until the end of life. When we come to Christ, we receive His heavenly food through listening to and reading the Bible, and then we will never be spiritually hungry. Well, I guess that is not a replacement for broccoli, baloney, and bagels, but spiritual food is certainly essential to eternal existence with God.

Therefore, perhaps we each need to take a moment and evaluate our spiritual diet. Burgers, brats, radishes, or their equivalent are a daily essential. Some of us can hardly go three to five hours without nibbling on a grape, chip, or salted peanut. Do we have the same craving for daily input from the Bread of Life? Set a goal to read a section of the scriptures and pray for at least a few moments daily. Share stories of Bible heroes with family. Crave a snack of Bible miracles. Enjoy fellowship with Christians around your table as you study the word of God together.

Rejoice that you are feeding your soul as well as your stomach. Appreciate His calorie-free soul food.

Did You Say, "Good Morning, God," Today?

Which Comes First?

Thanks to God for a safe, peaceful, stress-free sleep or
a cup of coffee, a frozen waffle, or a steamy bowl of yucky oatmeal?
As you leap or lurch out of bed, do you stop for a private word
with our Creator, thanking Him for dancing daffodils,
or do you just blindly scrub your teeth and wish the day was already over?
Did Grumpy Goof jump into your clothes or Grateful Grace?
Sometimes, Grumpy takes over my morning,
and prayers are ignored. Ugh.
Let's take a moment to peruse God's Word.

"Rejoice always, pray without ceasing, give thanks in all circumstances;
for this is the will of God" (1 Thessalonians 5:16–18 RSV).
"Shout for joy to the Lord, all the earth. Worship the Lord with gladness;
come before him with joyful songs" (Psalm 100:1–2).
"Oh Give thanks unto the Lord; call upon his name;
make known his deeds among the people.
Sing unto him, sing psalms unto him; talk you of all his wondrous works.
Glory you in his holy name: let the heart of
them rejoice that seek the Lord.
Seek the Lord, and his strength; seek his face evermore.

Remember his marvelous works that he has done; his wonders, and the judgments of his mouth" (Psalm 105:1–5 RSV). "But thanks be to God, who always leads us as captives in Christ's triumphal procession and uses us to spread the aroma of the knowledge of him everywhere" (2 Corinthians 2:14 RSV).

God seems to have several messages for us:

1. Rejoice, pray, give thanks always versus grumble, mumble, and pout.

2. Sing unto the Lord (in tune or off-key) with familiar hymns or modern Christian songs.

3. Tell others about the good things God has done. Stop right now and think of two blessings you experienced today. Personal testimony: I received news of a blessing God is working in the life of a friend as he struggles with bipolar challenges. God is also providing me with a clear head and thoughts as I compose this small essay designed to help each of us be more thankful. Pass on your joys and thanks to a friend through emails, notes, calls, or in person.

4. Yes, we can even talk about His wondrous works. Who did you share a wondrous work of God with recently? Were you given an extra week of life for which you need to shout praises? Did a family member come closer to Christ? Was a friendship strengthened recently so that the joys of being together may be renewed? Did you tell God how much you appreciated a recent sunset, flowering shrub, or fuzzy squirrel in your yard? (There are times, however, when I find it hard to thank Him for the crazy bunny who nibbles off our violets.)

5. Do you realize Paul tells us in 2 Corinthians 2:14 that God will cause us to triumph when we do things in His name? His name will be praised as you bake a berry pie for a neighbor,

open the church door for a stranger and smile,
or cry with a grieving friend.

**Reread the four scriptures quoted above.
Then my challenge to you:
Wake up each morning with thanks in your heart
and a cheery "Good morning, God!"
Shout it out loud.**

Foot in Mouth Disease

REMEMBER THE LAST TIME you put your foot into your mouth and embarrassed yourself? You immediately regretted the hurt you caused or the red face you suddenly wore. You mentioned going to a party and realized the other person had not been invited—ugh! Perhaps a comment about a friend putting on a little weight, when in reality the individual had a serious illness, causing both parties to feel uncomfortable. Having the tendency to say the wrong thing at the wrong time can be a problem.

James warned us about managing our mouth. We love to talk. Some say the average American citizen has thirty conversations in a day. We spend one-fifth of our life talking. In one year, our conversations will fill sixty-six books of eight hundred pages each. And now, this is the fun statistic (really): Men speak on the average twenty thousand words per day, but we women speak thirty thousand. No wonder guys often claim they can't get a word in edgewise.

Our mouths get us into trouble, causing us to stumble. We speak without thinking and hurt a friend. Disappointed, we grumble about others. Out of our mouth fly angry comments resulting in damage to a Christian worker or friend. We are unkind. The truth maybe is stretched just a wee bit. Perhaps we conveniently forget to add a fact or three, leaving an incorrect impression or idea.

Do you know anyone who has never let their mouth get them into trouble? Probably not. Each chapter of James reminds us of the need to control our tongue. The tongue can be a fire. We read, "Every kind of beast and bird, of reptile and sea creature, can be tamed and has been tamed by humankind, but NO human being can tame the tongue—a restless evil, full of deadly poison" (James 3:7 RSV). The venom of a snake can kill. Our thoughtless remarks may figuratively kill the spirit of whoever receives our angry words. Although James says the tongue can never be fully controlled, we certainly need to remain as vigilant as possible.

The tongue displays the real you. When we are full of love, joy, peace, and kindness, our verbal messages will reflect that. If our heart is harboring hurt, anger, jealousy, or just ordinary meanness, this will also be reflected in our speech. James again reminds us, "With it [tongue] we bless the Lord and Father, and with it we curse men, who are made in the likeness of God. From the same mouth come blessing and cursing. My brethren, this ought not to be so" (James 3:9–10 RSV). One moment we sing "Praise the Lord," and the next we are saying, "Shut up" (or worse). Our tongues become Dr. Jekyll and Mr. Hyde. Putdowns uttered from a parent's mouth, such as "You'll never amount to anything" or "You really are stupid," may damage a child's self-confidence for years. Asking for forgiveness is so very difficult but necessary.

Let me conclude by saying, controlling my tongue is a giant challenge. Today, I am writing to myself. If the message is appropriate for you, great. Then we can each pray for the power to control our words. We need to avoid putting our foot into our mouth.

**Get a new heart. Start over. Ask God for help daily.
Result: a kinder, more thoughtful you.**

Pass It On Alternative: A Generation of Bible Illiterates

RECENTLY, I JOINED FOUR cousins from across our country to review, investigate, discuss, and share information about our family. One cousin flew in from Oregon, two of us arrived from Illinois, and we were joined in the Boston area by two other relatives. Four of the group were dedicated sleuths, lugging along notebooks of detailed information gleaned from hours of poring over ancient letters, internet genealogy sites, and dusty cemeteries. Pictures of family members long departed from this earth cluttered our study table in the law office of Suze, my second cousin. Verbal stories and tales entertained us as we nibbled on sandwiches. We had to constantly remind each other of the relationships of various grandparents, cousins, or ancient aunts.

The fifth member of the quintet was the chief flunky. We will keep her identity secret, but she is currently penning this epistle. Although I loved hearing the tales, adventures, and misadventures of the Gray/Ransom tribe, I must admit that my skills and deep dedication do not include serious research of dusty files tracking down long-lost great-great-great-grandparents. My tasks included operating the copy machine, passing out coffee, and providing a pair of eager ears to listen to the stories of my relatives.

Now, you may ask, why in the world would five adults fill four days of their calendars gathering together to explore the lives of our family? Why should we invest in plane tickets, motels, rental cars, and a fresh seafood dinner? What motivated us to postpone our daily routines to join together for study, laughter, and hugs?

You guessed it: We wanted to pass on to the next generation the legacy of our family. Future Gray/Ransom folks need to appreciate the struggles and accomplishments of our tribe through times of war, peace, and movement from the East Coast to the West. It's important for the younger generation to know the heritage of successes and defeats of their family, as they mold their own lives and establish families. We learn from others' mistakes and victories. We desire that the next generation may know and honor our history. No illiterates wanted. We had a responsibility to pass it on.

As a member of the Christian family, I also want future generations to appreciate the struggles and blessings of followers of the Word. It has been stated often that the church is only one generation away from disappearing. Without knowledgeable, living examples of the teachings of Christ, some new philosophy may grab the attention of citizens of the future. We say we love the Bible and the message it proclaims, but how do we demonstrate that love? For many, the Bible sits on a shelf six days a week and is dusted off to carry to church, but seldom are the covers opened and the message read.

Think of your own family. Are they able to identify our Christian relatives? The early followers of Christ were the disciples. How many can your grandchildren identify? Can your own children relate the life adventures of Paul as he spread the gospel during that first century? When is the last time you read the stories of David, Abraham, or Stephen to the family as you gathered together around the table?

What about your own literacy program? Do you daily read a portion of scripture in order to feed your soul? Eating daily is a great habit of mine. Hamburgers, Brussels sprouts, or maybe even a jellybean are necessary to keep my physical body active. I must admit that some days, however, my spiritual body goes hungry. Without feeding and sharing with others, my religious muscles will become useless. I will be contributing to biblical illiteracy of future followers. Shame on me.

As a person of action, may I suggest a few positive behaviors we each might help activate:

- Initiate more frequent opportunities for all family members to read, study, and view the actual Word of God. Dust off the Bible. Download the Word on your electronic device. Copy favorite passages and adhere to a mirror for constant Bible snacks.
- Expect and support the belief that all church leaders must have solid, scriptural knowledge, basing their teaching or preaching on the Word, and not become sidelined with pop theology or trivia.
- Encourage many to accept the responsibility of teaching and the dedication that requires. Perhaps you too should teach. Introduce in your church the goal "Each One—Teach One."
- Begin daily devotions and experiment with in-depth Bible study with others, in small or large groups.

Don't let your relatives or friends think that Joan of Arc was Noah's wife, that Sodom and Gomorrah were married, or that the Sermon on the Mount was preached by Billy Graham. Let's encourage a biblically literate world.

Celebration—2018 Winter Olympics

Medals and Memorable Moments

SEVENTEEN DAYS OF SNOW, speed, and spirit are history, and 242 US athletes are home. Winners and the other athletes experienced cheers, parties, hugs, and yes, even some tears as family and friends celebrated. Memories will last and be shared with grandchildren many years in the future. The Olympics is a special time for participants as well as for family and observers.

The athletes incurred hours of training, endless bus rides, and security checks along with horrific winds and aching muscles. Jessie Diggins, who helped the US women win their first-ever Olympic medal in cross-country skiing, collapsed at the finish line. "I was in a lot of pain. My body is wrecked." In spite of being selected to represent their country and the joy of marching in the opening ceremonies, this was no cakewalk for our super trained representatives. For some, it was a life-changing experience.

Over fifty of our heroes arrived home with chunks of gold, silver, or bronze hanging from their necks. Hopefully, we acknowledge the dedication of each of the athletes, not just the ones standing at attention on a platform in celebration. Each of these trained, sacrificed, supported one another, and stretched their talents to the limits. In my book, they all deserve recognition and the right to feel the pride of accomplishment.

Our Christian life might be compared in some ways to the Olympics. The apostle Paul encouraged the young man Timothy to "train yourself in godliness; for while bodily training is of some value, godliness is of value in every way, as it holds promise for the present life and also for the life to come" (1 Timothy 4:7b–8 RSV). Timothy's coach, Paul, admonished him to train—train in godliness.

How do we do that? Prepare. Prepare daily in order to let Christ and God shine through all we do. To be godlike, we must let His image and personality be in our hearts. God is truth. God is pure and holy. His Son demonstrated love and sacrifice. Concern for others motivated Jesus's challenge to us. "But I say to you, love your enemies and pray for those who persecute you" (Matthew 5:44 RSV). To be full of godliness takes much practice, dedication, focus, and even sacrifice. These Olympians often found themselves in gyms and on ski slopes training long hours while their friends were tweeting, twiddling thumbs, or taking naps. To be godly is also hard work.

As we stayed glued to the news coverage, it became evident that all was not perfect on the slopes or trails. Among other challenges facing these winter heroes, I list a few:

- Strong winds blew some off course.
- Changing snow conditions as events were in progress necessitated quick responses.
- Stumbling, falling, or flipping in the air resulted in errors and exclusion from the winners' platform.
- Lack of focus saw men and women taking the wrong turn on the skiing slopes.
- Fear penetrated the hearts of some, especially when course conditions were less than perfect.
- Lack of family support resulted in discouragement. For example, one parent was heard to say, "My child could have done better." I cannot imagine how that athlete must have felt hearing those discouraging words. Incidentally, that athlete won a medal, in spite of the parent's lack of confidence and emotional support.

As we train ourselves in godliness, we face similar challenges. We, too, are blown about by winds that get us off our Christian course. The activities we participate in can quickly change our environment, causing us to stumble and fall. We take our eyes off Christ. Our focus blurs, and we experience trouble. Who has not been a bit fearful attempting to be

Christlike? And yes, sometimes even family members criticize their own children who are serving the Lord in magnificent ways.

"But those who hope [trust] in the Lord will renew their strength. They will soar on wings like eagles. They will run and not grow weary. They will walk and not be faint" (Isaiah 40:31).

Run for Christ.
Celebrate with family as together you praise Him who loves you.
You will be a winner eternally.

Kitchen of God's Word

A Series of Biblical Extension Courses for Use with People in Thailand

UNDER THE LEADERSHIP OF Mike Schrage, Good News Productions, International (GNPI), headquartered in Joplin, Missouri, has completed lessons in the Thai language especially for use in Thailand. The term "Kitchen of God's Word" refers to how pastors can use their own style and flavors to present the delicious truths as the learner feasts on God's Word. One of the first lessons deals with the value of salt. Just imagine the

references possible to leaders as they open the Bible. Here are three examples:

"You are the salt of the earth; but if the salt loses its saltiness, how can it be made salty again? It is no longer good for anything, except to be thrown out and trampled by men" (Matthew 5:13).

"Salt is good; but if it loses its saltiness, how can you make it salty again? Have salt in yourselves, and be at peace with each other" (Mark 9:50).

"Therefore, salt is good; but if salt has become tasteless, with what will it be seasoned?

It is useless either for the soil or for the manure pile; it is thrown out. He who has ears to hear, let him hear" (Luke 14:34–35).

"Let your conversation be always full of grace, seasoned with salt, so that you may know how to answer everyone" (Colossians 4:6).

Lesson leaders can take the selected scriptures and make appropriate applications for their audience. What might be some recipe variations for the above verses? This writer chose three possible themes. Will you now tweak, season, and add your personal applications as you become part of the Kitchen of God's Word? Remember: Salt adds flavor, is a preservative, and can be a healing agent.

Theme 1: Have You Become a Throwaway? Salt can become contaminated or tasteless. It is then useless. When do we as Christians become useless? Could our thoughts or actions contaminate us? Do we participate in sights, sounds, or activities that create unchristian moments in our head? If yes, what examples might pop into your brain? Ever know a follower who forgot about God's command to love everyone? Perhaps they love only those who fit their own group of friends but shut out those of different color, beliefs, size, personality, or economic levels? Hmm! Is age an excuse to become a useless throwaway? What are your thoughts?

Theme 2: Be a Peacemaker. Mark suggests we include "good salt" in our lives. How do we reflect a healthy, salted life? Our scripture suggests one way is by becoming a peacemaker versus a troublemaker. With whom do you need to make peace? A neighbor, family member, coworker, political opponent? How can we encourage our state and national leaders to become salty with a flavor of peace? Now you have a real challenge.

Theme 3: Discipleship Costs a Bundle. We look at Luke 14:25–35 to place our "salt" verses into context. Luke discusses the cost of discipleship. The suggestion is that we, the Christian followers, must give up our families and even our own lives. How in the world is that possible? Must I really hate my brother? Is my death essential to being a Christian? We are told to love one another, and then Luke suggests we hate family? Maybe we need a variation on the theme of hate. Perhaps the author is suggesting that we cannot love to the extent of idolizing our loved ones. Is it possible we could love family more than Christ? Would it be possible we spend more time making a child/spouse/friend happy rather than helping our family love the Lord and place Him first in our lives? How can we erase the fear of being a fruitful disciple and replace it with the goal to be Christlike?

My suggested challenge to you, dear reader, is to take one of these themes, read the passage carefully, and then think of personal applications. Share your thoughts with at least one other friend.

You, today, are the super chef in the Kitchen of God's Word.
Perhaps some readers would like to know more about GNPI.
If yes, go online to <u>enews@gnpi.org</u>.
My friends Ziden and Helen Nutt helped
establish this international ministry.

World's Largest Vertical Garden: Dubai Miracle Garden

AN INCREDIBLE FLOWER GARDEN is found in Dubai, United Arab Emirates. The garden opened in 2013 and occupies 780,000 square feet, making it the world's largest natural flower garden featuring over forty-five million flowers. You can go to the website (www.dubaimiraclegarden.com) or google Dubai Miracle Garden for an unimaginable array of pictures. The variety of arrangements, colors, and creativity boggles the brain. Reuse of wastewater keeps plants healthy as they pump in two hundred thousand gallons of water per day. The garden is open from October through April, skipping the summer months when temperatures are too hot for flower growing and gazing.

If we could survey photos of the garden, one giant observation would leap out—diversity. Flowers of every hue and color blend together to form the displays. We would witness blooms from tiny to gigantic. Included in the exhibition are short and tall clusters of color, fragile and sturdy buds, plants with a pleasant fragrance, and others with no scent. As the petals snuggle up together, one is reminded of the rainbow—God's creation. Alone, any one of these blooms is beautiful, but together, the medley of diversification presents an incredible spectacle. Differences create beauty, and God made it happen.

We as human beings (and as Christians) should take notice. God created people with equal diversity. Some are slim and trim, while others of us are tubby, lumpy, and plump. Colors of skin vary from pale to dark. Hair may be blond to black with many shades in between. Currently, the world has 6,909 registered living languages. Many folks believe in God, some doubt His existence, some reject His existence, and others haven't made up their minds about the subject. Introverts and extroverts, guns and gunless, Cards and Cub fans, and conservatives and liberals populate our country. No two persons are identical—not even twins. What a magnificent human garden of beauty and variety.

Is it time for each of us to celebrate that diversity and model our Dubai Garden? Can we perhaps begin to realize that we need each other? God made us each different, and yet He tells us to "Love each other as I have loved you" (John 15:12). The flowers grow and thrive as partners. At times, they even help another as one provides shade for a smaller bloom.

Do you and I each need to rethink what it means to live like a Christian in a world of diversity? This writer suggests that we do.

Will you join me as we review our attitudes and actions relating to this human floral landscape of diversity?

**Could we learn to love and support
others without totally agreeing?
Would it be possible to develop relationships with
someone from a different tribe or family?
Can we live in the same garden with those
from another side of town or country?**
Pray about it.
God says love, love even as He loves you.

Smile—It's Good for You

A BOLD HEADLINE IN the *AARP Bulletin* **shouted,** "To Prevent Flu, Smile? A Happy Mood Boosts Vaccine Effectiveness, Study Shows."

During the 2016 flu season, the flu vaccine performed well among adults fifty to sixty-five. The vaccine had no clear impact, however, on the health of people older than sixty-five. Apparently, their weaker immune systems reduced the effectiveness of the vaccine.

"We have known since 1996 that negative moods like stress affect how well vaccines work," says Kavita Vedhara, a researcher at the U. of Nottingham, England. Vedhara decided to investigate how mood might affect vaccine effectiveness. Great news: They found that while a positive mood, healthy diet, exercise, and lower stress all lead to an improved immune response, the biggest factor in how well the vaccine worked was the patient's mood on the day of the vaccination. Thus the title of this chapter: *Smile—It's Good for You* (AARP Bulletin, November 2017).

Wonder what the Great Physician has to say about this premise? God, speaking through Solomon, seems to understand the value of joy in your heart: "A cheerful look brings joy to the heart, and good news gives health to the bones" (Proverbs 15:30). What better way to demonstrate joy than sharing a brilliant smile, emanating from a genuine heart of love? Solomon, the brilliant king, produced many proverbs, or wise statements. He reminds us, "A cheerful heart is good medicine, but a crushed spirit dries up the bones" (Proverbs 17:22).

Perhaps Vedhara collaborated with Solomon—I'm teasing—as she studied his proverbs and ventured into serious research. A cheerful heart will produce a smile on your face and a joyful mood on vaccination day and then, hopefully, make the flu fly away for the season.

The problem, however, is how do we help folks have a cheerful heart? What causes genuine smiles to appear on faces? As you look at the various pictures on this page, you note that huge smiles are everywhere. Each of these folks certainly was in a wonderful mood at the time. One fellow is sharing his talents by cooking treats for friends. Another fellow is smiling as he is surrounded by balloons for a party. The third graphic shows a woman having a wonderful time at a birthday celebration. Folks hug, smile, share, and laugh. The smiles on various friends indicate they are obviously happy.

What were the elements of happiness? Celebration, sharing, having fun with a spouse, being part of a family that cares for one another, and building friendships with others. For at least this moment in time, cares, troubles, anger, loneliness or depression have been shoved aside. Their hearts and minds have been inoculated with pleasant thoughts. The common element for our friends in the photos is a smile. Paul anticipated the research study findings centuries earlier when he enjoined us to "be joyful always" (1 Thessalonians 5:16).

As children of God, we are immediately part of a global family. we can celebrate and rejoice in His presence every day and give thanks for gifts of life for each of us. He is our friend. Reach out to Him. Connect with His love. Accept His vaccination for our sins with His sacrifice on the cross, and you will smile.

Be prepared for a cheerful heart.
It's good for you.

Would Your Family Pay Ransom for Your Release from a Kidnapper?

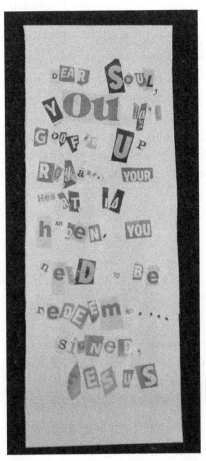

AS YOU READ THE question above, perhaps the adventures of Johnny Dorset will pop into your head. O. Henry's teasing 1907 tale, *Ransom of Red Chief*, turns the tables on a pair of amateur kidnappers. Needing cash, Samuel and Bill nab the only son of millionaire Ebenezer Dorset. Johnny is taken to a cave, and his father must come up with the kidnappers' demand for two thousand dollars in ransom.

Then the fun begins. Our young captive turns the tables on his captors. The ten-year-old is obnoxious. After he threatens all manner of dastardly actions toward his captors, including threats and pranks, the two decide to hurry and return Johnny to dad. They reduce the ransom to fifteen hundred dollars. But the father, who knows his son well, demands $250 of the kidnappers to relieve them of their captive.

You probably remember the conclusion of this ransom note. Criminals pay up. Son is returned.

We, too, were held captive, captive to sin with a death penalty on our heads. Then a wonderful event transpired. Our ransom was paid in full. "For what the law was powerless to do in that it was weakened by the sinful nature, God did by sending his own Son in the likeness of sinful man to be a sin offering" (Romans 8:3). "Just as the Son of Man did not come to be served, but to serve, and to give his life as a ransom for many" (Matthew 20:28).

The ransom did, however, have some conditions attached. Peter reminds us of a number of obligations including, "But just as He who called you is holy, so be holy in all you do; for it is written: 'Be holy, because I am holy'" (1 Peter 1:15–16).

This writer has no idea what ramifications our hero in the kidnapping event had to experience upon return to his father. I do know, however, that our Father continually heaps His love on us, His children.

Take a pause right now and mentally list at least six incredible blessings you have experienced in the past few weeks. What about an email from a longtime, misplaced friend? Maybe it is a doctor who discovered relief for your pain? Could it be that a family member whispered "thank you" for a kindness you delivered? Would your list include a new job, passing a test for completion of a unit of work, or just a hug from your dad or grand baby?

However, the important action now is to say thanks to our Redeemer. Then, reach out and share with a friend the joy you have in your life because of Christ's action. Invite that individual to consider letting the ransom be paid for his freedom from sin.

You must share your story.

Ransom Note

Dear Soul, You have goofed up royally. Your heart is hardened. You need to be redeemed. Seek me out, the lover of your soul. I paid your ransom in full, but you must accept. It will, however, mean life-changing behavior. Take action now. Signed, Jesus.

Lessons from a Grasshopper

Eat, Hop, Reproduce; What a Life

Grasshoppers are not creatures greatly to be admired.
Actually, people think of them as rather destructive.
They eat, hop around, and reproduce.
They do not contribute to the well-being of our communities.

IN NUMBERS 13:33, TEN of the dozen guys returned from spying out the Promised Land after the exodus of the Children of Israel from Egypt. They described the enormity of the inhabitants. They compared themselves and all of the Israelites to "grasshoppers." They were thinking about their physical size in relation to the natives in the Promised Land, but actually they were describing their own behaviors.

Throughout forty years of wandering in the wilderness, the Children of Israel constantly complained to God. They forgot about their miserable lives as slaves in Egypt. The memory of escaping through the Red Sea with the Egyptian army right on their heels was also forgotten. As they wandered in the desert, the presence of God guided them with a cloud during the day and a pillar of fire by night—and yet they complained.

They could not imagine what glories awaited them in the Promised Land. Moses's followers always wanted more. Food was necessary, but manna and quail did not satisfy their appetites. I guess they wanted a pizza parlor or a Dairy Queen. Complaints poured in, even though their clothes and shoes never wore out during the entire forty years of walking. These wanderers did not really want self-help to better their conditions. They let Moses and God do the work, and they just became consumers with a list of complaints. "The people sat down to eat and drink, and rose up to dance (1 Corinthians 10:7 RSV).

An estimated six hundred thousand men plus women and children left Egypt (Exodus 12:37). Only the two spies, Caleb and Joshua, were allowed to enter the Promised Land, as they alone had faith that God would deliver the land to them. Therefore, at the end of the forty years, we have an entirely new group of folks. Reproduction continued throughout their l-o-n-g hike. A new generation of about six hundred thousand men plus women and children entered Canaan (Numbers 26:51). They ate and gave birth like our grasshopper friends, but they also gave Moses and God a hard time with their constant complaining.

Are we any different today? Do we want to consume only the blessings of the Lord: good health, ample food, perfect grandchildren, and relaxing lives as we wait for the Promised Land in heaven? Have we been known to complain frequently about our jobs, church programs, government leaders, families, or health? Shame on us. We may be today's human grasshoppers.

On the other hand, what is wrong with consuming and reproducing? Haven't we been instructed to eat daily of the Bread of Life: His Word? John 6:48–58 reminds us that Jesus is the Bread of Life. If we come to Him, we will never hunger (John 6:35). The implication is that just as we require meatballs and asparagus every day, so we need daily spiritual nourishment. Heavenly food sources come from prayer and reading scripture. So we had better eat, or the church will be filled with anemic Christians (Acts 2:41).

In addition, what is wrong with reproduction? One of the last challenges Jesus gave to His disciples prior to His ascension into heaven was, "Go therefore and teach all nations, baptizing them in the name of the Father" (Matthew 28:19–20 KJV). With whom have you shared the love of Christ and His saving grace? Reproduce. Become a parent of a newborn Christian.

Becoming a part of the Kingdom of God is referred to as a "new birth": "I tell you the truth, no one can see the kingdom of God unless they are born again." (John 3:3) "If anyone is in Christ, he is a new creation; the old has gone, the new has come" (2 Corinthians 5:17).

We are newborns, new creations. We need spiritual food. We are required to bring others into the family of God. Reproduction is a requirement of a follower of Christ.

Birth, nourishment, reproduction. That is the cycle.

So, my grasshopper friends, go forth.
Read His Word.
Then encourage others to find Christ as their Father and Savior.

Just Passing By; Thoughts and Prayers

Religious leader or helpful Samaritan?
Sympathetic thoughts or involvement and dirty hands?
Which role do you usually play?

FOLKS AROUND THE WORLD of all beliefs seem to be familiar with Jesus's illustration of the Good Samaritan (Luke 10:25–37). Headlines shout out examples of people exhibiting kindness toward individuals in need. We view these stories of personal sacrifice and extreme efforts by young and old, and sigh, "Isn't that incredible." But what about you? Have you become a headline in God's Daily News of celebration?

Jesus responds to a question by an expert in the Jewish law, "Teacher, what must I do to inherit eternal life?" Love the Lord with all your heart, but also love your neighbor as yourself. Then the tough question: who is my neighbor?

The priest and the Levite publicly acknowledged their love of God, but they ignored the second half of the directive—love your neighbor. On the Sabbath, each would be found celebrating God. On this lonely, dangerous road, perhaps on a Monday, however, they had no time or inclination to interrupt their personal mission, become involved with an injured man, and care for his beaten, bloody body. Perhaps muttering a simple prayer, each continued down his own path of life.

A third person now becomes a part of Christ's narrative: the Good Samaritan. You know the rest of the story. He stopped, acknowledged the terrible situation, became emotionally involved, and took action. His own life was put on hold. He sacrificed energy, time, and finances. He cared and shared.

What about each of us? Is our religion a Sunday-only-worship-God experience? Or are we willing to put our life on hold for an hour, a day, or a week to care for ones in need, even if they're not from our world of family and friends? Can we initiate practical love wherever the need is found? That is the question Jesus wants us to consider.

Common excuses and rationalization seep into our hearts and minds when faced with tough decisions regarding true neighbor involvement and interaction. I'll pray, God, but here are some reasons for avoiding involvement:

- Others are more capable of assisting with the need. Call Hank or Jennifer to provide for physical, spiritual, or emotional needs.
- My own family and job require all of my time and energy. Sorry; no intensive caring from me.
- That is a dangerous neighborhood, and I might be assaulted. I think I'll pass on this opportunity.
- Let the family care for their own. I would be interfering if I called at the hospital, visited at their home, or bought a tank of gas (sounds a bit selfish, but ...).
- Since God hears my prayers, He will take care of the situation. If I pray, believing, He will pitch in without me.
- I have no idea what I might do to help. The need is so overwhelming, time-consuming, or unique. Count me out.
- Oh, my! I prayed and then got so busy and forgot to take a casserole over to share, or I meant to rake the leaves for the widow with a broken leg but was invited out for lunch, or I was going to call and lend a listening ear, but a friend stopped by and we talked for thirty minutes, or I had to work overtime for our vacation money, or the gift card I planned to send to help with expenses went for a new drill I wanted at home.

Are we so indifferent that trusting God to care for us as we care for someone in need is an impossible idea? Have we forgotten that love translates into action—not just kind words, thoughts, and prayers? Will we cheer others who sacrifice time, money, energy, and, yes, even safety perhaps, but we walk calmly by ourselves? Do prayers substitute for dirty hands or loss of private time?

> **You should interview your own heart today.**
> **Keep your eyes open. Be proactive for God.**
> **Help double the number of compassionate**
> **Samaritans in your town.**

So, You Think Fashions
Are Wild Today?

PERHAPS YOU, TOO, HAVE blinked your eyes twice as you glanced at the attire (or lack of it) of young people today. Has the sight of flesh showing a bit between shirt and shorts caused you to smile? What about those flip-flops or cutoffs at church? Do the wrinkles of unpressed jeans suggest a lesson in ironing is in order? Yes, I guess those of us over fifty have wondered a bit about today's dress code, sometimes with a smile, or maybe we just scratch our head and wonder.

Well, pretend you are reviewing a picture of four women taken circa early 1900s. If one of these ladies was to wander into our church auditorium on Sunday morning, I do believe our little eyes would pop right out of our heads. My first thought would be, "How in the world do ladies ever manage to bend their heads to pick up a child or scrub the floor with the stiff, tight collars?" Maybe that is why they look so somber in our mental picture. Men of that era were even funnier looking in their Dutch baggy pants and dress hats. Then I remember seeing a picture of my dad wearing something similar, minus black hat and wooden shoes, from around 1925–30. Clothes of that period were just not as comfy or casual as present-day attire.

Fashions certainly change over time—sometimes for the good, as we become more relaxed in our attire. I think back to the time of Christ as John the Baptist appeared on the scene. He was dressed in a desert garment made from woven camel hair and wearing a leather belt (Matthew 3:4). Smells a bit stinky to me. And then we read of the linen garments (cloths) in which Jesus was wrapped when placed into the tomb. According to historians, the body had probably been wrapped up like a mummy and covered separately with the napkin later found folded up in the empty tomb.

Clothes have been essential since the days of Adam and Eve and their goof-up in the Garden of Eden. Jesus reminds us in Matthew 6:25–33 to avoid worrying about "what you shall put on ... life is more than clothing." He takes care of the birds and dresses them in fine feathers. Surely, He will help us provide for our needs. Maybe not silver slippers, but at least a pair of leather sandals and a colored T-shirt.

The scriptures refer to clothing in a more symbolic way. In Matthew 7:15, we are told to be aware of prophets who come to us in sheep's clothing but inwardly are ravenous wolves. These folks, wearing misleading costumes of fancy words, are preaching false doctrine to the flock of Christians. Be prepared through knowledge of the scripture so you are not deceived by messages that tickle your ears but really do not rightly follow the Word.

What about the familiar scripture that relates to clothing—the famous "Put on the whole armor of God" passage in Ephesians 6:10–18? No need to dash to Walmart, Sears, or Talbots for this wardrobe. The only cost for these fashions is your willingness to stand up to temptation from Satan and surround your day with Truth. Add a layer of Righteousness. Your new shoes are called Peace. Then your outer layer of clothing is called a Shield of Faith. Oh yes! Don't forget that hat of Salvation along with a sword. (I know we don't carry swords today, but this one will not chop off heads.) Yes, the Sword of the Holy Spirit must be dwelling in you.

If each of us fully clothed ourselves with truth, right living, peace, and confidence in Christ, believing with a heart of faith, submitting to Him in salvation, and then allowing the Holy Spirit to reign in our heart, the world would be a significantly more likable place to raise our families.

Look around you. What do you see?
Are you pleased with the spiritually clothed
world your children will inherit?
If not, start by changing your own spiritual wardrobe.

True Friendship

Wisdom from Dogs, Cats, and the Scriptures

THE GREAT CARTOONIST CHARLES Schulz, creator of Charlie Brown, penned eight identifiers of the perfect friend (based on characteristics of Snoopy, the pup). My favorite was, "Always available to lean on and share a tear." As a cat lover, however, I have developed a few identifiers of their vacillating, feisty, feline friendship and love. The personality of the kitty probably is more reflective of human personality and constantly changing behaviors than man's best friend, the dog. What do you think?

Cat

1. Yowls for attention swiftly changes to purrs of contentment
2. Retracts sharpened claws to softened paws
3. Ignores owner for hours, only to suddenly plop onto your lap for a nap
4. Demands attention on her own time schedule
5. Claws delicate furniture but drops valuable feathered "presents" at your feet
6. Shuns strangers only to suddenly demand cuddling and petting
7. When snuggling with his human, focuses exclusively on said human and not on his phone
8. Ignores supercool cat toys, only to spend long moments with a single bird feather

But being **loved by a cat** is a "purrfectly" wonderful experience.

In the scriptures, we find many references of friendship provided by Christ. These reminders acknowledge that we, the consumer of His love, also are a vital part of the relationship. We must be proactive. Below are helpful reminders of the love responsibility of His followers.

Christ

1. "You are my friends if you do what I command you.… This is my command: Love each other" (John 15:14, 17).
2. "Draw near to God, and he will draw near to you" (James 4:8 RSV).
3. "Love one another with brotherly affection; outdo one another in showing honor [respect]" (Romans 12:10 RSV).
4. "A friend loves at all times, and a brother is born for adversity" (Proverbs 17:17).
5. The example of Ruth and her love for her mother-in-law: "Don't urge me to leave you or turn back from you. Where you go I will go" (Ruth 1:16–17).
6. "Greater love has no one than this, that he lay down his life for his friends" (John 15:13).
7. "Jonathan became one in spirit with David, and he loved him as himself" (1 Samuel 18:1).

Finally, what about actions of a human friend?

1. Sometimes steps out of her comfort zone to help or understand.
2. Does not require or expect reciprocal friendship but is overjoyed when a mutual relationship results.
3. Anticipates and initiates opportunities to share a laugh, hug, or giant listening ear.
4. Lets a friend share his weakness, sadness, disappointments, and even mistakes made in his life.
5. Prays consistently with and for a friend, both in person and in moments of silent, personal prayer time.
6. Sometimes envies the success of a friend, but then quickly celebrates his accomplishments.
7. Is someone you can be yourself with and never fear that she will judge you in good time or bad.
8. But sometimes friends (just like cats) do disappoint you. If so, the real friend will still reach out and hug.

Cats, Christ, and humans: We are each different, so choose your friends carefully and then carefully nurture that relationship. If you are friendless, get busy and initiate action to develop a friendship. Whether you're lonely, dog tired, or needing a cat nap, include Christ as your best friend.

Poverty?

When You Hear the Word Poverty, What Pops into Your Head?

HOMELESSNESS? BEGGING ON STREET corners? Shanties with corrugated roofs bunched together in a third-world country? Or perhaps we think of folks making less than minimum wage or receiving food stamps? Maybe the phrase "meager resources" pops into your head?

What should our Christian attitude be toward the poor? Shun them? Ignore them? Hastily look away? Smile at them but inwardly think, *Wow! I am glad that isn't my mother, uncle, or sibling*? Hopefully we are not guilty, but let's self-reflect.

Do we ignore hurting folks here in our own village, town, or church but collect large sums of money to be sent overseas to an African village? Do we pack our jammies and dash off to help the Haitian community but ignore our needy hometown neighbors? Probably each of us has ignored those in financial need, whether on a street corner or sitting in our own church pew. Guilty?

Today, however, we want to also draw your attention to other aspects of poverty. In some ways for both young and old, the poverty of being unwanted, unloved, or uncared for creates far longer-term scars and hurts than hunger. Envision in your mind a young lad. We'll call him Josh. He stands against the corner of an elementary school, wearing tattered clothes and holding a plastic lunch sack. His eyes are moist with tears as he huddles against the wall. It grabs my heart. Why, you ask? Let's create a second picture in your mind. Notice his classmates walking by, chatting with each other in their spiffy clothes and fancy backpacks. No eye contact with Josh. No reaching out to his loneliness. Probably no offers to join the ballgame, sit with them at lunch, or come to a birthday bash. Undoubtedly, Josh is even the target of kid bullying.

Being ignored can be crushing to the soul of young and old. How often have you seen children and adults sitting or standing alone? Perhaps they are first-timers at church. What action do you take?

Humans were made by God to need friends—to communicate with others. God made a helper so that Adam would not be alone (Genesis 2:18). Loneliness is deeper than sitting home alone cheering as the Cards subdue the Cubs or eating a burger by yourself at the local fast-food venue. Certainly, we each cherish moments alone. Voluntary solitude is a great time for reflection, prayer, restoration of our energies, or a catnap.

Our Josh, however, is surrounded by students and teachers all day. His solitude is not voluntary. This guy is eager to be part of the gang. It reminds me of recess time, when ball teams were being selected. Maybe you even remember being the last kid called for team membership. Scars of unwanted last for years for some.

His emotional discomfort stems from not being included. Friends don't voluntarily ask him to a neighborhood hot dog roast. No one notices his tears. Loneliness is partially self-imposed, as Josh subconsciously knows he is not just like the others, but the stress is real. The emotional scars are lasting. Adults, too, secretly cringe at the thought of entering a church service knowing no friendly smile will greet them with a bit of conversation above the obligatory "Hi, how are you?" Maybe they even inwardly long to join a group for lunch, to be a partner in a calling group, or to receive a friendly phone call. Okay, dear reader. Have you been guilty of quietly walking by our Josh in the hall, too busy catching up on the news with your friends that the stranger in your midst is missed? We each are part of the solution to the lack of inclusion, which is a form of poverty.

Christ, however, acknowledges a third group who are poor: the poor in spirit. In Matthew 5:3 we read, "Blessed are the poor in spirit, for theirs is the kingdom of heaven." What do you know? Christ wants us poor—poor in spirit. Yuk. But yes. We need to recognize and acknowledge our spiritual needs and reach out to His Word. Just as the physically hungry seek bread, so must we seek the Bread of Life. The self-righteous will be found wanting.

Contrary to what my little brother said as a lad, "Own self do it," own self cannot save oneself. The Kingdom of God will be ours as we submit to His leadership and beg for help. Hard for some of us to do.

There is poverty everywhere.
Open your eyes and reach out to help, but also
acknowledge your own spiritual poverty.
Connect today with one lonely soul.

A Daisy Delight in a Sea of Concrete

Christ in the Middle of New York City: A Blessed Find for Worship

FOR A NUMBER OF years, a group of friends and I have made an annual trip to the Big Apple. We enjoy a week of shows, admire the art, taste special yummy treats, and have a wonderful time in the city that never sleeps. It takes at least twenty-four hours to adjust to the constant noise of the 8.5 million folks as they move around New York City's blinking lights, screeching sirens, and tooting horns.

Sunday arrived that first year, and I knew I wanted to worship and celebrate the Lord's Supper. Would that be possible in this concrete jungle? Wonders of wonders. As I exited the elevator in our hotel a block from Times Square, I spotted a bulletin board listing churches in the area. Scanning the board, my eyes jumped when seeing a small card announcing the site of West Manhattan Church of Christ. The address seemed close enough to walk, so I set out. Hiking about twenty-five minutes, I watched for a church sign. Nothing. After passing the address, I returned looking more carefully and discovered a simple door in the middle of the block with the correct address. Poking its head through the concrete by the door was a tiny daisy smiling at me.

Opening the door, I found myself in a small room with about twenty chairs, a couch, an ancient piano, a simple table with preparations for the Lord's Supper, and a podium. Bible study was in progress, but the leader stopped, invited me to be seated, and introduced himself, and I responded in kind.

About ten or twelve folks smiled at me. Several were Asians. And so my first worship in New York began. As we sat there, I was amazed. The door would open and a street person would arrive, sit for several moments, perhaps help himself to a doughnut, and then wander out. Other worshippers would drop in and drop out, but through it all, the program proceeded with spirit and dedication. The message was straight from the Word of God. I was so blessed to be a part of an inner-city gathering of Christians. I return each year and find the same wonderful Christian fellowship.

The question rushes through my brain: how small is too small for worship? The answer, of course, is, "Where two or three come together in my name, there am I with them" (Matthew 18:20). Today we applaud megachurches, where multitudes are receiving spiritual food weekly. This is praiseworthy, but have we mentally erased from our memories that the early church met in homes? The gospel spread from Antioch to Athens without gospel bands or paid workers. The Word can change lives whether it is explained to twenty or twenty thousand. Dedicated leaders reaching out to members of the family of God with sincerity and love are the key to pleasing God, not the size of the crowd or the polish of the leadership.

Perhaps you, too, may find yourself near Fifth Avenue some Sunday. I invite you to wander over to 443 W. Forty-Ninth Street (between Ninth and Tenth Avenue) and break bread with fellow followers of our Savior. You will be blessed as you uncover the **Daisy in the Asphalt.**

Undeserved Gifts: Preparing Our Hearts for the Greatest Gifts of All: Love, Grace, and Salvation

WE PREPARE FOR THE Christmas season in many ways. The lighted deer and twin trees shine brightly in our yard. A bag of Christmas cards stares me in the face as I anticipate writing the annual Christmas letter, while filling my brain with memories of joys and sorrows of friends of the past. Some folks love to drag out the crafts and create imaginative treasures to share with others. Trips are planned. Others work long hours serving and selling goods to eager shoppers. Hopefully, time is also spent sharing the gift of Christ and His story with family as they gather to eat the fatted calf or stuffed goose.

As the twenty-fifth of December creeps up on us, however, I have grown increasingly aware of another outcome of this season: fear. Fear that there will be no turkey and dressing for some family. Uncertainty regarding gifts for the children fills the hearts of many. Depression occurs in the minds of others as loneliness, unpaid bills, health issues, or the stark reality of uncertainty for the future faces them. Poverty in the midst of plenty has truly stared me in the eyes recently as I viewed our community. Wow.

How can this happen? What should a Christian do? Who should we encourage, comfort, and support while attempting to care for our own loved ones? How can each of us personally connect in a time of severe need? Is it possible to wake up my insensitivity for those crying for help? Christ recognized the hungry and provided a feast from five loaves and a couple of fish. When the storm threatened the disciples' boat, Jesus calmed the seas. He reminds us that when we feed and care for those in need, we are really showing our love for Him.

I have heard these commands all my life, but have I really listened? How much love should we share? When can we quit? Or can we ever stop? He demands our all. Yes, even when exhausted, you reach out again.

God demonstrated His love for us, in that "while we were still sinners, Christ died for us" (Romans 5:8). That is giving until the end. Can we do less? Maybe it even challenges us to give not only to those in great need but also to our enemies. Check your Christmas giving list. More than family? Friend or unknown with giant needs included? What about a family member or casual acquaintance with whom you have had conflict this year? Where are they on your "caring for others" list?

Forgiveness of our sins is, we must admit, an undeserved gift from God. Rethink your options. Involve the family in a time of sharing with others. Occasionally give without letting the left hand know what the right hand is doing. Go beyond the expected. Perhaps even give to someone not appreciative of your generosity. Remember also that we actually own nothing. It is truly the Lord's, and we are His caretakers. So take good care.

Love and share. "Little children, let us not love in word or speech but in deed and in truth" (1 John 3:18 RSV).

The Christmas Doorstep Challenge Is On

Imagine how many homes could be brightened by a simple gesture. (Could be any special day—Thanksgiving, Easter, Mother's Day)

The Rules

1. Find a single mom or family on welfare or someone with extensive medical bills. Look around for a retired couple who are seeing their savings dwindle and could use some cheer. Maybe your minister needs a bit of encouragement.
2. Choose a gift—big or small. Maybe even homemade, or a gift card.
3. Write an anonymous note, including kind words about why you are thinking of them. If appropriate, add an invitation to drop in to your church. Watch for them and greet them.

4. Leave the gift or note on their doorstep or mail the gift card, minus your name.
5. Knock on the door and leg it—make sure they don't see you!
6. Go home and pray for your secret friend(s).
7. Feel blessed knowing that you have spread some Christmas cheer with no expectations of anything in return. Include your children in the experience.

**Model and start the habit of sharing early
in the life of each family member.
Let's share and see if this catches on and we can spread
a bit of Christmas magic. Miracles really do happen.**

Based on thoughts by Caroline Macro.

New Beginnings

Welcome to a New Year—A Year of Opportunities

Satisfying or Sad?

- 365 days to share God's love with others or sit and eat plum pie
- 8,760 hours (including sleeping) to be Christ's light to the world or shut our eyes
- 525,600 seconds to pray, be kind, cry for a friend, chase the kids, or play golf

What do you plan to do for the Kingdom this year? No excuses now. Each reader of this book has some talent, ability, or skill and sufficient energy to reach out to someone else.

- Connect with that neighbor, newcomer, lonely mom, high-paying executive, or angry kid who needs a listening ear.
- Invite a stranger from church to have a cup and conversation at your favorite beverage shop.
- Smile and shake the hand of a guest near you in the pew. Tell them how happy you are they are present. Look them in the eye and encourage them to have a wonderful period of worship. You will be surprised what that means to a first-timer. Especially

watch for someone who seems a bit nervous, awkward, bashful, or alone.

- Stitch some quilts, work for the food bank, send a text, visit a hospital patient, drive someone crazy, but do something for the Kingdom. We need to keep active.
- Form a small group and study the Word, pray, make coffee cakes for the church staff, take asparagus salad to someone hungry, or rake the widow's yard—but work together—love each other and ask a lonely one to join you. Teamwork is an effective way to build relationships.
- Find a Christian book or article to read and then discuss the main idea with a friend(s). This is how we learn, just like Christ: He taught the disciples and then sent them scurrying off to share the Good News with others.

The apostle Paul made a complete new beginning after his encounter on the road to Damascus (Acts 9). First, he had a simple name change from Saul to Paul. Then, it was an occupational change from slaying to praying for Christians. How dynamic a new beginning was that? Few of us will experience such a makeover.

Later, however, Paul reminds us, "Therefore, if anyoneis in Christ, he is a new creation; the old has gone, the new has come!" (2 Corinthians 5:17). When we acknowledge Christ as our Lord, our lives must change. We are now God's servants, fulfilling His will. Occasionally, however, we mortals forget that metamorphosis in our lives and revert to old habits and attitudes. January is a wonderful opportunity to recommit.

New Year's resolutions are easy to make but difficult to keep. Weight Watchers' business accelerates during January, but soon smoothies, sundaes, and giant salami sandwiches ease back into our diets. Likewise with Christ. We promise our families increased love and joy. Our hearts and minds tell us to go the second mile in helping others, but shortly, our body engine runs out of motivational gas. Helping hands become motionless. Inertia slows, and the Kingdom work is neglected. So much for new beginnings.

Today, I challenge each of us to renew our dedication and become that new creation. Make it a time of new beginnings.

Listen for the Bell

MERRY OLD ENGLAND HAD some crazy practices, as evidenced today in our language. Life in the 1500s was stressful. From these days of Shakespeare, we commonly use phrases such as "It's raining cats and dogs" and "Don't throw the baby out with the bathwater." The background of three such phrase comes to mind as I think of the church.

England is quite small. By the sixteenth century, burial spots had become scarce. People began to dig up coffins, take the bones home, and reuse the graves, so the story goes. As they opened some of these containers years later, they found scratch marks on the inside. One out of twenty-five coffins contained these marks, and suddenly, people speculated what was happening: Folks were being buried alive. This was apparently a result of drinking their whiskey or ale from lead cups. When combined, it could knock you out for a couple of days. Family would assume their loved one was dead and so conduct a burial service when, in fact, they were just sleeping off their time of frivolity.

Upon realizing this, a custom began of tying a string onto the wrist of the "deceased." This string was then led through the coffin and up above the ground, where a bell was tied on the end. Someone would sit in the graveyard all night to listen for the bell. That is how the phrase "graveyard shift" began. If the bell rang, the person on the graveyard shift would know that someone needed to be "saved by the bell" or he was a "dead ringer."

As I reflected on this practice, my mind leapt ahead to today. As Christians, we must learn to listen for these bell-ringers. Maybe you know someone who is figuratively buried alive in their home. Perhaps they are inactive, watch hours of TV, or slip in and out of church with their presence barely acknowledged. Life encases them in a sheltered box of loneliness.

They are breathing youth or adults with potential for engagement, excitement, and mental stimulation. Although solitude and reflection are important, interaction with others is vital for a full life. How will we, as Christians, let our light shine for Him if we are buried within ourselves?

Jesus zipped off into the wilderness for prayer and quiet time with His Father. But He returned to teach, coach, comfort, and prepare His followers for future witnessing. So also do twenty-first-century Christians need companionship, action, and involvement. Acknowledging Him as our Savior requires us to then to live a life of witnessing and sharing. Perhaps we as members of the Christian family need to tune our ears to their silent ringing so they may be saved by the bell.

Can we each take the graveyard shift? Let's reach out to these silent dead-ringers. No, they are not physically deceased, but metaphorically, they are barely breathing. I challenge each of you reading this to tune in to friends or acquaintances needing to be saved by the bell. Invite them to church, Bible study, or just for a cup of java. Visit, call, or encourage them to help with meal preparation for a church function. Challenge a lonely person to tutor a student needing help with his history lesson. Both individuals will reap benefits. Help a young lady make a connection with the music director who can recognize she has talents that are needed by the Lord. Provide warmth and a hug, when appropriate, to a weary mom. Invite a lonely teen for a bike ride, hike, fishing trip, or a visit to a local museum. Be proactive as you quietly extend an arm of friendship.

**Remember, the church either continues to grow or it dies.
As part of the body of Christ, we cannot just stand still.
Ding-dong, the bell is ringing. Do your part.**

Family Time

Napoleon Bonaparte said, "Show me a family of readers, and I will show you the people who move the world. If you want your children to be intelligent, read them fairy tales. If you want them to be more intelligent, read them more fairy tales."

What do you think?

READING IS IMPORTANT. WHEN I was young, our family constantly read books aloud. I still remember my father reading *Treasure Island* to us around our fireplace. Library cards were ever-ready companions at our home, regardless of where we moved, which as a child was very frequent. Today, I still have two books that my aunt Eleanor gave me when I was a wee one. My professional career centered around books and helping folks become more competent readers and teachers of reading. Even now, most evenings, I curl up with a book prior to flicking off the lights. Yes, reading is important in my life.

What about your family? Do you share books and stories together as a family? Perhaps today's story time becomes CD time while traveling in the car. What better way to experience the joys of pirates, habits of wild animals, or the latest challenges as an Olympic swimmer? Books also instruct, bring tears, solve problems, or carry you into a world of fantasy. As parents read, so do their children. Kiddos model the adults in their lives, whether cooking, scuba diving, volunteering to help others, rock climbing, or being grumpy. So be a reading model.

But what about Napoleon's comment that if you want your children to be smart, they should read fairy tales? *Little Red Riding Hood, The Three Little Pigs,* and *The Billy Goats Gruff* wandered around our home. Yes, we read fairy tales, but is that the way to get smart? Maybe, but this writer would suggest that also reading God's Word might be more helpful than tales of Goldilocks or Cinderella. How might that happen?

The Bible inspires. As we read about the Good Samaritan helping someone in need, we're challenged to lend a hand to someone hurting. David finished off the giant with five pebbles. Maybe you, too, can conquer giants of despair or anger in your life with God's help and prayer. Stephen so loved the Lord that he was willing to give his life for his friend. Paul was challenged to work with the early church and thus became a model for missionaries. You, also, can be inspired to serve.

The Bible encourages. Paul said, "If God is for us, who can be against us?" (Romans 8:31). If that is true, we should be ready to tackle any challenge before us. Workers for the Kingdom are in constant demand. Your mind speaks to you softly, saying, "No, I have no talent." Accept the promise that He will be with you. Participate in the music program, help corral three-year-olds, or host a small group for in-depth Bible study. Pass out bulletins, clean up the church auditorium after service, or be a Sunday greeter. Read about fishermen who became brilliant spokesmen for the Lord as Jesus directed them to "go into all the world" and reach out to others. Then do likewise and encourage others to join you.

The Bible instructs. As we read the scriptures, we find ways to improve our character and change our behavior. Hebrews 4:12 says, "For the word of God is living and active. Sharper than any two-edged sword, it penetrates even to dividing soul and spirit, joints and marrow; it judges the thoughts and attitudes of the heart." Wow. Look out; you may need to make changes in your life. For example, read together John 6:1–15. Then as a family, discuss what lesson we might learn from the lad's generosity as he shared his fish and quintet of rolls? Continue to share His Word at least once each week. As you read, encourage each family member to think of applications for today and then follow the directions and guidance Paul and the other writers provide.

So how can you help your family become a family of readers? Read yourself. Read to your kids and grandchildren. Find wonderful videos and CDs of religious as well as secular stories and listen together. Have younger family members read to you while you share a cookie or a carrot. Download or buy books for gifts. Talk about Bible stories and help make them come alive. Listen to stories of Old Testament heroes as you drive to Grandma's house. Create mini family dramas of favorite Bible stories. Use scripture to help solve family challenges. Show the family the Word is important.

You may not become a mental Napoleon,
but reading will enrich your life.
You can be a family of readers who moves the world.

Dropout or Follower? Which Are You?

THE SILENT EPIDEMIC; ARE you a part of the dropout generation? Students leave school. Adults abandon jobs. Children are left with a single parent. Even seniors vanish from society to isolate themselves in their bungalows, surrounded by memories and miseries. What is happening? Why are folks abandoning responsibilities and relinquishing commitments? What does this commentary mean for a Christian?

In October 2007, Pastor William Chaney wrote "The Silent Epidemic: Perspectives of High School Dropouts." He shared the top five reasons high school students drop out, based on an extensive survey and interviews. From this research, perhaps we might explore reasons for today's dropout culture. What did students say?

47 percent said classes were not interesting.
43 percent missed too many days and were unable to catch up.
43 percent spent time with people who were not interested in school.
38 percent had too much freedom and not enough rules.
35 percent were failing in school.

Let's look at these five excuses. Could there be lessons for adult dropouts—dropouts from church, from commitments, or from other responsibilities at church, work, and home?

1. **Interest** was of top importance to students. Perhaps our generation tunes in to only novel or entertaining content. Are you guilty of mentally dozing while listening to a sermon or class lesson? The Sunday morning alarm drags you from your dreams. You turn over, start to climb out from the covers, and then you think, *Oh,*

it's chilly [windy, rainy, snowing, beautiful, too hot, too whatever].
I'd rather spend time doing something I enjoy than sit and listen to
a sermon. Others disappear from worship because the music is too
loud or too soft, or they are unfamiliar with the hymns. Guilty?

2. **Absent too much** results in dropouts. Each time, Mr. or Ms. Adult,
   that you stay home, say no to involvement, or become too busy to
   bother with church, it gets easier and easier to say no. The high
   school student falls behind in work. Lessons don't make sense, so
   the assignments require increasing energy and time. That is not
   much different than the absentee adult from church, work projects,
   or even class parties. Your mind becomes filled with other events
   and activities. You begin to subconsciously feel ill prepared for
   the Sunday lesson. You find new friends far away from the church
   pew. You drop out.

3. The students, while absent from school, **spend too much time
   with other dropouts**. Together, they bond and encourage each
   other to avoid school. Likes attract. It's no different with adults. As
   you spend more time with folks not engaged with Christ and His
   church, your interests shift. Meetings, friends, yard work, hobbies,
   and parties fill your life away from the Kingdom community. The
   balance of activities tips, and suddenly you realize that you are a
   church dropout, just like a high school kid.

4. **Too much freedom negatively influence participation.** When
   just doing my own thing, it became increasingly difficult to
   tolerate rules and structure. Retirement brought freedom from
   goals, timelines, specific responsibilities, and "have-to" rules. As
   a worker, you had to dress appropriately, be on time, complete an
   assignment, read uninteresting material, and stay off your cell
   phone. Life now is simpler and more enjoyable when there are
   few (or no) rules to follow, or at least the teen thinks that is true.
   Are you different? God has set up guidelines of behavior for His
   children. He says purity and modesty are appropriate behavior.
   We are to love our enemies, share with the poor, place Christ first
   in our lives, and give from our hearts of love. Now, we say that is
   just too many rules, and so we just disappear from serving Him
   and live our lives like we want. Sounds like a high schooler to me.

5. **The dropouts were failing in school**. No wonder. If they skipped
   class, failed to listen to boring content, or spent time with other

dropouts enjoying their freedom, they were bound to fail. If we quit participating, reading, and studying unless it is fun, we'll find ourselves failing when God comes to call His own. If we have spent no time with Him on earth, why would we expect to be with Christ for eternity? All Christians must continually grow, study, work, and extend our energies in outreach because we love Him. The Lord compares those of us who hear the Word but do nothing to the guy who builds his igloo on the sand. When the storms of life arrive, the house is washed away (Matthew 7:24–28). Dropping out is not an option for Christians desiring to live with Christ for eternity. You will get an F on your report card.

Don't become a dropout. Connect with Christians. Get busy.

Dropout or Follower? Part II

Lead the Way and Become a Follower

THERE ARE TWO DOORS; which do you choose?

Door 1: Dropout. Isolation, loneliness, self-pity, feelings of worthlessness, or even depression

Door 2: Follower. Serve, care, help, cry with a friend, change diapers in the church nursery, or share the message with others of good things that happened to you as a follower of Christ

The previous essay discussed the concept of dropping out. Hopefully, as you considered the downside of isolation and inactivity in your relationship with the Lord, you are ready to try door number 2: being a follower.

Followers don't sit on the sidelines. Imagine yourself as a follower of a political candidate or a supporter of a public cause. You get engaged. You take time from your schedule to participate in rallies, walks, office work, calling, preparing mailings, or whatever is necessary to promote your position or public figure. You are willing to get your hands dirty or sacrifice time with your family to carry the message to others in your neighborhood or social groups. Your T-shirt identifies your affiliation. Generally, it is no secret who you are supporting and giving your time and energy. In fact, you are such a follower that you invite others to join you. You become a follower who leads.

How does this correlate to our relationship with Christ? How can we be followers who lead? That sounds like an oxymoron. Let's think about a

Christian follower and leader. Paul has some suggestions in 1 Corinthians 2:1–5:

1. **Come with humility.** "When I came to you, brothers, I did not come with eloquence or superior wisdom as I proclaimed to you the testimony about God" (vs. 1). Even Paul, the super leader, maintained a humble heart. A follower of Christ recognizes that He is God and we are His children. We obey, not argue, thinking we know it all. Humble is the word. (Hard for some of us when we receive earthly applause. Big heads can result.) "I have been crucified with Christ; it is no longer I who live, but Christ who lives in me; and the life I now live in the flesh I live by faith in the Son of God, who loved me and gave himself for me" (Galatians 2:RSV).

2. **Stay focused.** "For I resolved to know nothing while I was with you except Jesus Christ and him crucified" (vs. 2). Leaders for the Lord avoid getting sidetracked on diversions of the moment. They teach and model Christ and His sacrifice. Are we as followers too easily sidetracked with popular events or causes and spend little time sharing the stories of the Bible with our grandchildren and friends? Is love for the unlovable absent from our lives? Do we shy away from folks different from ourselves, whether economically, physically, or socially? Does skin color or cognitive ability hinder our outreach efforts? If yes, we are off focus. Followers model Christ's focus on spreading the message of love that His Father sent Him to deliver to the world.

3. **Acknowledge fear and weakness.** "I came to you with weakness and fear, and with much trembling" (vs. 3). Yes, it is okay to be afraid or timid as a follower. No one says a follower of Christ cannot be a tad nervous when asked to pray in public or take communion to a shut-in. Shaking hands with strangers can be intimidating. Paul says even he was shaking with fear when he spoke to the church in Corinth. What? Do you think you are better than Paul? He just knew the Lord had a mission for him, and he got to work. So must you acknowledge your need to get active, take off the dropout button, and fasten on the follower pin.

4. **Speak from power of the Spirit.** "My message and my preaching were not with wise and persuasive words, but with a demonstration

of the Spirit's power" (vs. 4). Yes, you need to continually study the playbook: the Bible. The time will come, however, when you must speak out, demonstrate, or model His teaching and love, and then the Holy Spirit will provide you with wisdom and power. Wow. That is a relief. A follower does not have to be an orator, a charismatic speaker, or a genius. The power of the Spirit will leap out from your soul, and hearts will be touched with His message, not yours. You were just the follower sharing—and yes, you were also being a leader, telling others about your Leader. See how easily we slipped from being a follower to being a leader?

5. **Represent God, not self,** "so that your faith might not rest on men's wisdom, but on God's power" (vs. 5). When the president's press secretary person speaks, she is not representing her own thoughts or opinions, but those of the president. You, too, as a follower/leader, are not promoting self but Christ. The mirror in your life must reflect His face, not yours, when reaching out to others. It is not your brilliance or talent but God working through you.

So how are you doing as a follower who leads others? Dropout days are history. Start being an active follower.

In closing, I want to share the testimony by LaMarcus Aldridge of the San Antonio Spurs. Perhaps it will inspire you to lead as a follower of Christ wherever your life takes you. Aldridge plays power forward for the Spurs. Hear his moving words: "I came from poverty and a tough household where we didn't have enough money to really eat, to where I am now. I know it was God giving me the guidance. I am one of His children, and He's let me glorify His name with my game" (*Oregonian*, April 23, 2014).

You, too, can be bold.
You, too, have a message to share with someone. Get going.

Incredible Christian Witness

Former NFL Heisman Trophy Winner

DURING THE JULY 2016 North American Christian Convention in Anaheim, President Dave Stone, senior pastor at Southwest Christian Church (Louisville, Kentucky), interviewed former NFL Bronco quarterback and Heisman Trophy winner Tim Tebow. For non-football fans, Tim is the young quarterback who bravely witnessed his faith while on the field. During the interview, Tim shared actions of the Tim Tebow Foundation and what he sees God doing around the world through the foundation.

> Tim also shared his inspiring personal philosophy that
> I challenge each of us to take seriously ourselves.
> "I believe God wants to use us," he said,
> "but we have to step out and say,
> 'God, whatever you want to do, I want to do it with you.'"

What about each of us? Have we stepped out on the field and heaved a touchdown pass as a witness for Christ? Are we willing to acknowledge God publicly, or do we quietly attend Sunday services and then put our Christian uniform back in the locker for six days? Most of us will probably be reluctant to paint a scripture verse under our eyes, as he did, but what scripture have you shared this week with a hurting friend? Do your neighbors or best friends experience your Christian love as you listen when they are experiencing pain or loss?

Did you remember to share a scripture along with your favorite corn casserole you delivered at the time of a co-worker's loss or hurt? Perhaps, next time, add a sticky note to your banana bread gift of love. The note might say,

> "The Lord is close to the brokenhearted and saves those who are crushed in spirit" (Psalm 34:18), or "The Lord is my rock and my fortress and my deliverer, my God, my rock, in whom I take refuge, my shield, and the horn of my salvation, my stronghold" (Psalm 18:2), or "So do not fear, for I am with you; do not be dismayed, for I am your God. I will strengthen you and help you; I will uphold you with my righteous right hand" (Isaiah 41:10).

What about your own family? Are you smiles and joyfulness for everyone all day, but at home, Mopey Molly? Do your children, spouse, or grandchildren think of you as a "Sunday-Only Christian"? Does your impatience with everyday family occurrences cause you to erupt like a volcano with a flow of unkind words or stony silence?

If our children were asked to describe their parent's most outstanding characteristics, what would be their reply? "My mom was a wonderful cook, and her cherry pies melted in my mouth," or "My best memory of Dad is when he took me golfing or camping." Wouldn't it be wonderful if the answer was, "My parents led me to Christ and daily modeled for me what a loving Christian does for everyone with whom they meet. They were my Christian example and yes, we also went biking together."

Tebow's public actions on the field were cheered by many, but others found it offensive as he bowed and gave thanks for a successful play. The apostle Paul and many first-century followers of Christ were persecuted for their observable faith. Some were stoned, placed in prison, or killed. Are you as courageous as first-century followers or Mr. Tebow?

Does a Christian witness require very public manifestations? Painting a scripture verse on our faces, as Tebow did, is not mandatory. We must, however, help folks around us be aware of our faith. Talk about your personal relationship with God. Share your struggles and how your faith helped you cope. The struggles you've experienced in life are what allow you to have compassion for those who are going through a hard time. Be authentic, not stiff or pompous. Be intentional and take the initiative as you share what John 3:16 means to you.

Above all, be genuine; don't attack or make fun of someone, but
step out and say,
"God, whatever You want to do through
me, I want to do it with You."

Facing an Epidemic Loneliness

THE MORNING PAPER'S OPINION section had a startling comment by George Will, editorial columnist. With wonder and sadness, I read the headline: "How to Heal our Epidemic of Loneliness?" Could it be true? Are Americans really lonely in large numbers? Writer Will states a number of facts, including the idea that Americans are richer, more informed, and more connected than ever, but more unhappy, disconnected, and isolated than previous generations. Some would suggest that loneliness is the number one health crisis—not cancer or heart disease. The studies suggest that loneliness is as physically dangerous as smoking fifteen cigarettes a day. Loneliness accelerates our cognitive decline. Lonely folk often die younger. Ugh.

Apparently, even though most of us are continually connected to folks from sea to shining sea, we are missing something. Home entertaining is frequently replaced with sharing pasta at Jim's Italian Garden. Virtual friends replace over-the-fence conversations and connections with the family next door. Checking our phone occupies office and theatre break times. Time spent in sharing family stories and concerns with colleagues, visiting senior citizens in care centers, or clipping coupons together has vanished like fog on a sunny morning. Our social infrastructure is crumbling.

Could this really be true? My mind slipped into reverse, recalling seventy years ago when I grew up in a small town in rural Missouri. What was happening then that produced connections or fertilized relationships? Ah, I thought. Spit and whittle corners: corners on the main drag where several guys would stand, whittling away and chewing their tobacco, while comparing high school sport heroes, pickup truck innovations, or the latest grain prices. Service club members created haunted houses, had fundraisers for community needs, and spent hours together as friend to friend. Talking time was in person, not skyped.

And yes, what about those church basements, where moms would drag the little ones by the hand and spend the morning around a large piece of cloth stretched over a frame, dipping their needle in and out, in and out? Beautiful patterns appeared on the quilts, but laughter, chatter, and gossip also entertained the ladies, binding them together in friendship. Other days, the ladies would bake a batch of chocolate chip cookies, carefully wrap them in wax paper, and then knock on the door of shut-ins. How those seniors enjoyed a few moments of human contact and conversation, Of course, nibbling on the cookies after the ladies left was a pleasant replacement for their dry morning toast.

Friends shared chores, had backyard hot dog roasts for the gang, visited over the picket fences, or shared in harvesting the crop of an ailing farmer. Kids' birthday parties centered in your home with balloons, pin the tail on the donkey, and fluffy chocolate cake, rather than at Pizza Hut or a bounce house. Friendly challenges engaged the gang in baseball rivalries. Porches held rocking chairs and hammocks designed for summer relation-building conversations with friends. Jobs were relatively stable, creating bonding between employees and employer. Life truly ran at a slower pace. Result: We knew each other. We knew someone cared. We built relationships.

So what happened? Friendships, of course, still develop today. Activities with fellowship thrill the heart of participants, and notes are sent to the lonely, albeit often online. Friendships happen, but with much less frequency. A home-cooked meal for friends is almost as rare as dogs eating pickles. Seniors live longer, often alone or in simple rooms in a senior care facility. Families, spread out across the country, are no longer handy to take Grampa out to the kids' soccer games. Factories close, stores go bankrupt, technologies replace loyal, dedicated workers. Relationships are weakened and replaced. And so the headline: "Loneliness Epidemic."

Now, as a Christian, this is disturbing news. What would the Word suggest we need to consider? Paul urges the Romans *not* to "conform any longer to the pattern of this world, but be transformed by the renewing of your mind. Then you will be able to test and approve what God's will is— his good, pleasing and perfect will" (Romans 12:2). Are we taking on the mind of modern society, isolating ourselves in technology, concentrating on individual desires and pleasures, and ignoring the swirling world of lonely folks around us? When is the last time you had a meaningful conversation with a neighbor three houses down the street, or with a hurting, grieving, struggling acquaintance? Have you shared a joke, worry, photo, or recipe in person rather than through technology? If not, why not?

Loneliness vanishes when you feel needed. If that's true, you must help discover connection points for the lonely to activities that will not only make your community a better place but will help eradicate the **loneliness** epidemic. Step up and step out of your own comfort zone and identify at least one person with whom you can be a difference maker. Model for your children the spirit of connections and service. Transform your own mind to be like Christ.

Be bold and share a valuable commodity, friendship, with at least one lonely person.

New Year Resolution: Pray

ESTABLISHING NEW YEAR'S RESOLUTIONS is not a habit in my life. To be honest, I don't believe I ever jotted down a goal for a New Year. I don't know why. Too busy? Too knowledgeable about myself to know I would never keep it anyway? Regardless, 2018 was a leaf-turning year. I made my first-ever resolution—to change my prayer routine and consciously, daily, and intentionally find private moments to chat with God. The following six principles guide me in my prayer life:

Pray Daily

You are a member of a family. You share the same home. At mealtime, the family gathers around the table to share the chicken soup or pumpkin pie. Bedtime arrives, and all head off to sleepy time. There is a big problem. Throughout that day, barely a word, other than an occasional request for something (e.g., "Pass the butter" or "Where is my sweater?"), was ever spoken. What is wrong with this family? No conversation with each other. No sharing of joys, trials, information, or even compliments. As an outsider peeking into this family, one would wonder about the silence. Now stop and think. We as Christians are members of a family. We have a Father. We are His children. Have you chatted with God today?

Are we treating God in a similar manner as the family just described? When is the last time you prayed, other than to perhaps ask for a simple favor or to give thanks for a meal? God, I need help with my bills. Please send me twenty-four hours of pain-free knees. Oh, but you say, I thank Him occasionally, maybe once a week. Yes, this morning I complimented

Him on a beautiful sunrise. But, you say, I just don't have time to have a brief visit with Dad each day. I am too busy living my life. Do you think our Father might like to have more conversations? Try a daily appointment with God. Celebrate or share joys and worries. Compliment Him. Thank Him, and, yes, make petitions for others.

Pray Intentionally

"But in everything by prayer and supplication with thanksgiving let your requests be known" (Philippians 4:6b RSV). My resolution includes being as specific as possible as I pray. When I'm tired, I slip into global phrases like, "God, heal everyone. Please make the world safe for Christians to spread the Word. Thank you, God, for helping families in our church with needs." Yes, I pray, but so nonspecifically. Take time to think about an individual with a need. Then pray for them not just by name but with their family in mind. What do they need? When is the surgery? Pray for the doctor. Think carefully and let God know. Pray specifically. Pray repeatedly. Pray expecting God's will to be done.

Pray with Power

"When you pray, you must not be like the hypocrites. For they love to stand and pray in the synagogues and at the street corners, that they may be seen by others. Truly, I say to you, they have received their reward. But when you pray, go into your room and shut the door and pray to your Father who is in secret. And your Father who sees in secret will reward you" (Matthew 6:5–6 RSV).

Pray Believing

Pray quietly. Powerful prayers do not need to be flowery or elaborate. Be sincere and simple. With sincerity, let your requests be known to God. Basic prayer time will be alone, just as Jesus prayed alone in the garden. Public prayer must be expressed in a humble way.

Pray Conversationally

Pause occasionally and just chat with God. Share your joys, thanks, petitions, cares, and burdens, but also listen to God by reading His Word as you pray. One-way conversations are usually self-centered, boring, and nonproductive. Sharing of needs, listening for guidance, praising the Lord, or even tearful petitions will be more satisfying when the petitioner stops and listens to God speak through the Holy Spirit. Remember, this is conversation, not elaborate, fancy words. Let your heart speak.

For example, are you exhausted from Christian service volunteering, balancing family needs with hospital visits, or preparing lessons for the nursery class you teach weekly? Does the thought of writing one more note to a hurting friend almost send you into tears? Then stop! What did Jesus do following enormous pressure from speaking to thousands, healing the sick, as well as coaching His interns? "But Jesus often withdrew to lonely places and prayed" (Luke 5:16). Perhaps you, too, need to sag back in the recliner and breathe deeply. As you relax, whisper a prayer for personal renewal, guidance, and new focus. God will be listening, just like He did when His Son called on Him in times of stress.

Pray and Act

You pray for a family in need. Time elapses. Nothing seems to happen. A drone does not land on their doorstep with a care package. The children are still hungry. Mothers huddle with the wiggling ones in their cars with temperatures below zero. Why didn't God hear and reach out and help them? Stop and wonder with me. Is there a second step in this action? We reached out to God, specifically asking that the family be fed and find housing. We prayed, believing. But then we just sat and waited for the problem to be solved. Oh-oh. All talk and no follow-through. Help sometimes needs action on the part of the petitioner. Did we forget to help find housing? Did we make calls to an inner-city mission for suggestions for the family? Did you provide a food card for use at the school cafeteria for the children's lunch? Don't expect God to do it all. He sometimes needs worker bees on earth to help carry out His plans.

You, my friend, may be that worker bee.

Friendship, Love, Faithfulness

Through Joyful Days and Stormy Seas

PERHAPS AS WE EACH begin new phases in our lives, it is time to inventory our relationships and actions with our loved ones. There is an oft-told story about faithful commitment to a special person.

One morning, an eighty-year-old gentleman was making a hurried visit to his doctor around eight o'clock. Arriving at the office, he encouraged the doc to speed his checkup along as he had another appointment at nine o'clock. The fellow added that every morning he needed to hurry to the hospital to see his wife. Upon inquiry by the doc, he added that his wife was diagnosed with Alzheimer's disease over five years ago. Even though she did not recognize him anymore, he faithfully paid his daily visit.

The doctor then inquired as to why he made those visits if she had no idea who he was. The reply was, "Because I still know who she is." This is true love and friendship.

Did you identify some worthy qualities of this eighty-year-old? Three thoughts are shared here. Perhaps you have additional ideas.

Love

The promise found in many wedding messages to love and care for this person "in sickness and in health" is demonstrated. What about your own marriage commitment years ago? Does love still shine through, even in times of stress? Are you willing to step out of your comfort zone because of love? What new demonstration of your love might even cement that love relationship even more? Think creatively and then implement. "I am my lover's and my lover is mine" (Song of Solomon 6:3).

Tenacity

Morning after week after month, a nine o'clock trip through heat, snow, sprinkles, and perhaps with arthritic aching joints. Would you be that faithful? (Besides, the senior care center might not even serve your favorite hash browns and fried baloney with over-easy eggs.) "Love is patient, love is kind" (1 Corinthians 13:4).

Unselfishness and Giving

Each day, his wife was first in his life. Undoubtedly, he greeted her warmly. A hug, kiss, or just a touch of his hand on hers, but connecting daily with the love of his life. For about 1,825 days, these expressions of caring and giving were extended to a person not responding, not acknowledging his presence, not even calling him by name. She was lost in a world of her own, and yet he came. Don't you wonder if he might rather have enjoyed a second cup of coffee with the guys at the doughnut shop? What about sinking down into his rocker and reading the ridiculous news of the world? Was there not a TV show, book, or gathering of fellows that might also be tugging at his heart for attention? Yet each day, there he was—giving of himself for her who knew him not. Love "always protects, always trusts, always hopes, always perseveres" (1 Corinthians 13:7).

Well, what about God? Is He not also faithful toward his children, day after endless day? His arms are ready to reach out, even to those who were once His but have faded away. Today, so many no longer acknowledge Him as their lover. He is faithful. Are we? Do we visit God daily in our conversational prayer time, or have we drifted mentally away from Him? Perhaps we do not even remember His name (except maybe in moments of anger or frustration). Do we reach out to His children who are fragile, failing, or in care centers? Yes, it might be inconvenient, but God needs His healthy children to love those who may even be unable to respond with voices of thanks. Stop and think. If the tables were turned, wouldn't you want someone to care enough about you to visit, hug, or help? Shut-ins often are lonely. Please care. "Give thanks to the Lord, for he is good. His love endures forever" (Psalm 136:1).

Time now to think about it as we continue
into the future left for us.
He still knows who we are. Are you remembering who He is?
Love demands work, forgiveness, sacrifice, and sharing.

Surprise

DURING A TRIP TO New York City, we paid a quick visit to the Metropolitan Museum of Art. Knowing rain was threatening, we hurried up to the roof lookout area for a glimpse of the city skyline. As we walked out of the door, our eyes took in the new exhibit: a wonderful old home that had been carefully reconstructed on site. The entryway was so inviting, I was tempted to enter immediately, despite knowing one never touches an exhibit.

As we meandered around to view the city outside, I uttered a laugh. What had appeared to be a perfectly constructed, livable home was only a shell. Outward appearances from the front were authentic, but in back, only a simple metal structure held up the facade. How disappointing. How misleading.

Matthew 23:27–28 came to mind: "Woe to you, scribes and Pharisees, hypocrites! For you are like whitewashed tombs, which outwardly appear beautiful, but within they are full of dead men's bones and all uncleanness. So you also outwardly appear righteous to men, but within you are full of hypocrisy and iniquity" (RSV). Christ must have been sadly shaking His head as He viewed the robes of the religious leaders and heard their conversations. He peeked right into their hearts and saw—not metal pipes holding up their frame, but dead men's bones inside a handsome casket. Those religious fellows looked holy and powerful on the exterior, but inside they were dead because of unholiness. Their hypocrisy was identified and criticized by the Master.

So what about those of us today who call ourselves Christians? If we looked into the mirror of our lives, what would we view? Respectable on the exterior, but ugly thoughts in our hearts? James makes an interesting comparison in James 1:23–26. If we hear the word but are not a doer of the word, we are similar to one who views herself in the mirror and then just walks away, forgetting what she looks like. Do we hold blue ribbons for perfect attendance or liberally quote scriptures, but our heart is full of anger or our tongue lashes out with cruel words toward others? We read the scriptures but fail to apply the charges for Christian behavior as we meet the public day and after day. Shame and a sham.

How might we describe a religious hypocrite today? Perhaps one who attends services weekly but hops into the car and is immediately unkind to family, business associates, or casual contacts? Maybe it is a person who proclaims loudly that God loves everyone and yet shuns folks who do not match up to his social, economic, political, or ethical standards? Have believers failed to remember to "love the person" while still politely acknowledging that some behaviors are inappropriate for a Christian? Do we say, "God loves a cheerful giver," but fail to share our time, talents, dimes, and energy for Kingdom work? Everyone has exhibited hypocritical attitudes or behaviors at one time or another. So I guess we have been that "pile of dead bones" inside a beautifully decorated casket.

We need to avoid being fake Christians. Our faith and love must be demonstrated consistently for all contacts, at all times. People judge us on the outside for either good or bad, but God's x-ray eyes probe inward to our thoughts and hearts. We must be the real deal. It's tough being a Christian 24/7, but the Pharisees were criticized for failing consistency, both outward and inward. Beautiful smiles, kind words, and tender actions must not be matched with a self-centered, "me-first" attitude. The Christian life is more than believing. It is a way of behaving. The true follower is more than talk and intellectual knowledge.

Our hearts must also be in tune with the ultimate conductor of our lives.

I close with a simple wartime story of a Christian who lived her love:

During war time a Turkish soldier chased a brother and sister for some distance, finally killing the brother. The sister is captured and put to work as a nurse in the hospital of the enemy. Some weeks later, as she tends the wounded, she recognizes one of the patients—the killer of her brother.

What should she do? She could ignore his life-threatening condition and just walk on to another patient, or she could tend to his needs. She has only moments to make a decision before life will end. He recognizes her as she contemplates her choices.

Her mind is made up. She tends to his wounds, and after a few days, he has recovered. As they are about to part, he asks her, "Why? Why were you willing to save my life when I took the life of your brother?"

Her response was swift. "Because I serve Him who said, 'Love your enemies and do them good.'"

And then the most marvelous comment from our injured warrior: "Tell me more of your Lord. I would give anything to have faith like yours." What a marvelous witness.

Are you a reflection of Christ 24/7?

Are You Starving Yourself
to Death? Yes or No?

ONE IN THREE ADULTS in the United States is considered obese, according to a 2016 Gallup-Healthways poll. Diet plans consume our news media as they advertise another magic solution for losing weight. Folks feel guilty for avoiding Silver Sneaker centers stuffed with cumbersome exercise machines thrashing away, attempting to slim you down. Pounds are a problem for many.

But could it be true that we are starving in America? Certainly, there are parts of our city, country, and world where lack of food is a real challenge.

The picture below taken in a hut found in Hwange, Africa, demonstrates levels of poverty we cannot imagine, compared to a sausage shop in Athens, Greece, where an abundance of meat tantalizes our taste buds. While in the small African homestead, we discovered that the family could not afford to buy diapers or soap for their newborn. Yes, many are physically hungry, but that is not to what I am referring.

Don McMinn has a weekly on-line newsletter; in one essay, "Cultivate Your Intellectual Nutrient Base," he has another take on starvation and death. He boldly says, "People who have pushed the pause button on their personal development may be described by the fictitious gravestone that reads: 'Died age forty-five; buried age seventy.' Quite frankly, those people are uninteresting and lifeless" (March 30, 2016).

Folks who are fully alive, current, and vitally engaged with life are interesting to be with. Go and do good, plant pansies, hunt tigers, stroll in a park, read a new mystery, share your hobby or talent with a fatherless kid, bike a mile (or ten), create a new menu item for the family, listen to Mozart, paint the house, vigorously discuss alternative ways to save money for your local taxing body. Keep yourself connected with friends and the world, even if confined to a chair or bed.

My longtime friend Nancy K., although in extreme physical pain, still writes letters of encouragement to others. She wants to keep busy. It helps her not think of her own pain. Although I agree 100 percent with the need for each of us to continue to be intellectually engaged and active with the world around us, that is not the entire point of this essay.

What about starving ourselves spiritually? Christians need to be alive and vigorous in our relationship with God. Our Bread of Life comes from daily feedings from His Word. When is the last time you had a scriptural meal? Our eyes may become dim. So no excuse. Listen to scripture and messages online, by radio, or on TV. Does your spiritual head and heart resemble the meager cooking/kitchen area of the African home, or is it crowded with messages of love, faith, hope, and anticipation of His coming, much like our sausage store?

Grab your Bible and study. Read Christian articles and then have a mini-lesson with a friend as you share the ideas presented. Go to www.wschurch.org and listen to sermons by Eddie Lowen. Stretch the brain with Bible topics you've never explored before. Wrestle with spiritual ideas in your study time with a Bible buddy. Exercise the brain by reviewing tough Bible questions (e.g., Where do we go when we die?). In Philippians 3:17, Paul encourages the Christians to imitate his behavior. What might those actions be that others should replicate? This mental exercise and sharing is necessary to avoid obesity of the mind, just as physical exercise keeps one slim and trim. The result will be healthy, interesting, engaging Christians sharing their love with others. We want no biblical headstones reading:

"Died age forty-five. Buried age seventy."
Instead, what about this gravestone?
"Died at age seventy while reading Revelation 21."
Praise the Lord.

Who Caught the Big One? We, Not I

MY HEART IS BEATING rapidly. A giant smile covers my face. As I climb into the small ocean craft, my eyes sparkle with joy. The day is finally here. I am going to experience my first-ever deep sea fishing adventure. The owner of the small craft knows I am excited. We start out one beautiful, sunny morning for an adventure of my lifetime. As we cruise out of the harbor, we bait the poles and attach them to the sides of the boat. We sit back to wait. Will we be successful? What will it feel like to tangle with a large fish? Minutes pass. Although we are enjoying the rocking of the

little boat and the scenery, there is no action. Thirty minutes, forty-seven minutes; they stretch into sixty-plus. My smile diminishes a bit. I slump down and think, *Well, God, at least we can see your world from a different perspective this morning.* But I do add a bit wistfully, *Lord, it would be so great to catch a big one.*

Suddenly, there's movement at the back of the boat. The assistant grabs a pole and begins to tug and pull. An object is shoved into my hands, and the captain yells, "Down, up, reel! Down, up, reel!" I clutch the rod and picture in my mind fishermen turning that little handle with great speed—with the line coming in rapidly. Is that happening with me? Absolutely not. The pole is heavy. The drag on the line feels like a baby whale. The cranking is not smooth. In fact, I can barely turn the handle.

The captain continues to holler, "Down, up, reel! Down, up, reel!"

I hear him, but I'm not able to fulfill the job. I try to bend forward and back and crank, but believe me, it does not go smoothly. We lose the fish. Disappointment fills my mind. Will I have another chance? Yuk.

About a hundred minutes into our trip, action begins again, and once more, I do my best to follow the directions. I turn and turn the handle. My arms ache. I worry we will lose again. Then a miracle: The assistant leans over and helps with the turning of the handle. We work for several more minutes, which seemed like an hour. The splashing fish is almost at the boat. And then, we have captured her. A flopping fish before our eyes. A mahi-mahi, eight to ten pounds of beautiful colored fish lying on the deck.

We reach shore. Pictures are taken. The fish is given to the captain. Then I begin to reflect. Jesus and His disciples had a similar experience in Luke 5. After an entire night of fishing, nothing. Help arrived. Jesus said, "Throw your net on the right side of the boat and you will find some" (John 21:6). Result: a giant pile of squirmy fish. What was the difference? Help arrived. The guys could not do the job alone. The great Fisher-of-Men had to assist. They needed help, just as I did.

How often have we started out to do a task for the Lord (e.g., comfort, counsel, or cast out the Bread of Life to a friend), and it seems like there's no response? We struggle to make connections or meaning for our listener. Our faith gets tired, and our heart aches. We become impatient. Giving up even enters our mind. I'll just go sip tea and try another day to share the love of God with her. And then we remember: God is there to help. The Holy Spirit can provide us with wisdom. Pray silently for guidance and appropriate words. Just don't give up. Faithfully keep on keeping on; it's essential for positive results.

**Friends need to join hands with us to serve
the Kingdom. We need to be patient.
Time is on God's clock, not ours.
I cannot do it alone. We must join hands with God.
So today, dear reader, will you also go fishing?
Remember, though, to take the Lord along.**

Limpy Daisy Duck

EARLY ONE SPRING MORNING as I drove down our lane, I spotted a pair of mallards crossing the road. Springtime makes even the ducks' hearts' grow fonder. Slowing down to allow their safe passage, my eyes were drawn to something not quite right. Papa was safely within the trees, but Daisy was moving ever so slowly. After looking carefully, I noticed she took a step with her left foot but then could hardly follow up with the right. Step—limp—step—limp, she walked on. Then my eyes spotted the problem. Her right foot was bent slightly outward. She was injured.

Did she quit? No. Cry out? Not a peep. She continued until finally reaching her male companion. Perhaps several little ducks resulted later from this journey. We saw her several times in the days that followed as she slowly plodded along. How frustrating her life must have been. Each time, however, her faithful companion was by her side.

I thought of Limpy Daisy recently as I recovered from knee replacement. Following surgery, you either decide to stay prone in bed or breathe deeply, stand up, grab your cane, and move forward—limpy, limpy, limpy. As I continued my hobbling, medical personnel or a friend were nearby, waiting to help if needed. How I longed for the energy to leap over tall buildings or at least over sidewalk curbs. Perhaps Daisy, too, longed to return to the water, where swimming must have produced less hobbling and faster forward motion.

Regardless, we each plodded forward—duck and lady. Perseverance and a team concept produced advancement, though not necessarily pleasure. A community built on relationships provides encouragement, helping hands, and support. Maybe it was just a phrase from my friend saying, "Let's try those exercises one more time." (Granted, she sat in the chair with her cat-of-nine-tails ready to snap into action if I failed to grudgingly comply with the directions.) Sometimes the support meant bringing the ice bag or fixing a favorite snack when my appetite vanished. Friendship was really solidified when she set her alarm three times during the night in order to bring proper pain meds that first evening home. How does one express appreciation for such friendship?

The Kingdom also needs to build relationships and support from fellow Christ followers. Helping others should not be a burden but a blessing. Charles Dickens suggested that "no one is useless in this world who lightens the burdens of another." Booker T. Washington's slant on relationships resulted in "Those who are happiest are those who do the most for others."

But what about the scriptures? Jonathan, King Saul's son, became David's friend. Jonathan then attempted to persuade Saul, his father, not to kill Dave. Afraid, however, that Dad might still pursue David, Jonathan warned his friend. They make a covenant of friendship, even to the extent of hiding his warrior buddy from his dad. Perhaps you, dear reader, might want to review this extreme example of building relationships with folks as then, together, the will of God can be extended. 1 Samuel 18–24 provides the narrative of this special friendship between the king's son and a loyal warrior and future king.

The Lord constantly reminded His followers to share: "If you have two tunics, share one with one who has none" (Luke 3:10–11). "Love one another as I have loved you" (John 15:12). James tells us to visit orphans and widows in their affliction (James 1:27). And, of course we have the wonderful passage, "Greater love has no one than this, that someone lay down his life for his friends" (John 15:13).

The real message today, however, is building true relationships or friendships. Is this act possible in today's society? We constantly scurry and hurry, hither and yon. Everyone is in a hurry: hurry to work, get kids to school, answer our social media accounts, or just get home to our planned evening of movie reruns, reading, or an early evening nap. Who takes time to call a friend, checking on her health? When have you invited a lonely soul to share a cup of soup or coffee at a local deli or around your kitchen table? Finding volunteers for major, multi-week commitments as youth sponsor, class teacher, or even driver for the church bus is almost impossible today. Why? Perhaps we are too much in a hurry to fulfill our own pleasures and wishes. Is this what the Christian community needs?

How do we build relationships resulting in sharing and caring for others? Christians have to stop and step out of their comfort zone. Greet and meet strangers at church. Offer to take them to the coffee area or to your class. Introduce them to the ministers. Help register the children at the youth center. Drop a note later that week expressing your joy in greeting them. Become part of a class or small group sponsored by the church. Help chop onions in the church kitchen for a youth chili party. Reach out. Connect with others.

Appreciate the joy that results from caring for another.
Find someone limpy who needs your hand of love.

"Ho-Hum" Philosophy: Are You Guilty?

IT HAPPENS DAILY: WE turn the water faucet on and assume safe, clean liquid will pour forth. We hop in our car and anticipate driving over decent public roads. Flip the light switch, and brilliance floods the room. We give little thought to how these services work. We panic, however, when results are negative.

According to the guest column by Fred Coombe in the May 16, 2016, *State Journal-Register*, "As Americans, we take for granted our public infrastructure and the workers that maintain these systems." Despite what we often think, our transportation, water, electricity, and waste material systems are among the most reliable in the world. Our ancestors paid dearly to fund these projects designed by talented engineers. Why do we grumble and complain when a severe storm knocks out the power for a short time? Letters to the editor criticize public officials when potholes cause bumpy driving. Seldom, however, do we send notes of appreciation to these engineers or public works officials thanking them for clean water, efficient electric sources, or adequate roads upon which to drive. What is wrong with us? Occasionally we are mad or upset, but we continue to just assume these services will always be available. Ho-hum.

Perhaps, however, we should also look in another direction. What else might we take for granted? The air we breathe? Changing seasons, rain, carrot crops that thrive annually, and birth of new folks made in God's image? We pray expecting peace, health, anger control, or safety for loved ones. Do we just assume that God will supply our every need? I can hear us thinking, *Ah, God did it again*, without really showing appreciation.

What would we do if God decided to take a year's sabbatical and leave us on our own? Maybe that would help us overcome our "Ho-hum" attitudes. No dandelions to pull, streams for fishing, or air to breathe. That would get our attention in short order.

Peter tells us in 1 Peter 5:6–7, "Humble yourselves, therefore, under God's mighty hand, that he may lift you up in due time. Cast all your anxiety [cares] on him because he cares for you." When is the last time you remembered to thank God for caring for you? Malachi the prophet reminds the Children of Israel with these words: "'I have loved you, says the Lord.'" In Psalm 55:22, we read, "Cast your cares on the Lord and he will sustain you. He will never let the righteous fail."

I challenge each reader to daily join David with his prayer: "I will praise you, Oh Lord, among the nations; I will sing of you among the peoples. For great is your love, reaching to the heavens; your faithfulness reaches to the skies. Be exalted, Oh God, above the heavens; let your glory be over all the earth" (Psalm 57:9–11).

Remember the story of the healing of the ten lepers on the border between Samaria and Galilee? Ninety percent of that lucky group who gained their health just took for granted that some guy (Jesus) along the road allowed them to join society again. Only one recipient (the Samaritan) said, "Thank you." Even Jesus wondered where the other nine fellows were (Luke 17:11–19).

How ungrateful can people be? Surely none of us would have failed to show our appreciation to the Great Healer if we had been one of the ten. Or would we have? What blessing(s) did you take for granted in just the past twenty-four hours? Are you thankful for a roof over your head? Does your family bring you joy as you worship Christ together? Did the glow of the sun make your strawberries sweet and juicy? What about the everyday robin, fresh air, or multicolored daffodils waving in the breeze? Who do you really think made those beauties and joys happen? The Great Creator provided for His children. Now, say thanks. Yes, right now as you are reading this little essay.

Wake up your brain. No more ho-hums.
Replace your take it for granted philosophy
with a spirit of gratefulness.
Swallow some "I-will-always-give-thanks" pills.
Praise the Lord daily. Start today.

Things We Say Today Which We Owe to God

SHAKESPEAREAN PHRASES HAVE SLIPPED into our everyday speech, without most of us even realizing it. Who among us has not referred to someone as the "laughing stock" or argued for "fighting fire with fire"? When asked how I feel, I often reply, "Oh, so-so." Many common expressions were created by this prolific author.

As I reviewed some of them, I thought about the scriptures. God, through His followers over the centuries, has also provided us with thoughtful expressions to guide our lives. With "bated breath" I began a little search. Perhaps it would be a "wild goose chase" but it was worth a try. I have "not slept one wink" since I began my search of the scriptures and I have vowed not to grow "fainthearted." "For goodness sake," there should be numerous phrases we use ever so casually.

Hitting "Google," I searched for famous religious quotes. That was almost a "wild goose chase," but we will share what we found. "Have faith as a grain of mustard seed" (Matthew 17:20 RSV). "Well done, good and faithful servant" (Matthew 25:23 RSV). "Pride goes before a destruction [fall]" (Proverbs 16:18a). I like "labor of love" as found in 1 Thessalonians 1:2–3 (RSV) when Paul commends the Thessalonians for their faithfulness and labor of love. Wouldn't it be great if the Master one day says to you, "I commend you for your labor of love"?

Maybe you are attempting a fund-raiser for the Kingdom with a goal of $400,000. At the end of the pledge session, you have $2,000; we say that is like "a drop in the bucket" of our goal (Isaiah 40:15). "A peace offering," or "a multitude of sin," or "a nest of vipers"—each come from the scriptures. Who has not referred to someone as a "thorn in my flesh" (2 Corinthians 12:7 RSV)? Paul used this term to describe some challenges given to him. I love his reasoning. "And to keep me from being too elated by the abundance of revelations, a thorn was given me in the flesh, a messenger of Satan, to harass me, to keep me from being too elated." That is one way to help us not let pride consume us. Maybe you, too, have a thorn in the flesh.

We also are "guilty as sin" of cliché abuse. How often have Christians said, "I was born again" or "I was saved"? How often do we "greet one another with a hug and a holy kiss"? You have undoubtedly said, "Bless your heart," or "God works in mysterious ways his wonders to perform." From His Word? Nope. Not from the Bible. Maybe your favorite phrase is, "Share prayer requests," or "He's on fire for God," or "We'll be praying for you." They each are perfectly appropriate phrases, but not from the scriptures. My mother used an expression frequently, "If it's God's will," I will be there or do that. Again, not a Bible quote. Appropriate thought, but a human invention.

Oh, well.
If it's God's will, I will be back again with another thought.

What Are You Reading? Part I

Just for Fun Survey

AMAZON RELEASED A LIST of one hundred books to read in a lifetime. I have read at least a tenth of the list, including *Alice's Adventures in Wonderland* and *Angela's Ashes: A Memoir by Frank McCourt*. Then I wondered what I've missed by omitting the other eighty-eight or ninety titles from my reading experiences. Probably very little. The article went on to present a list of guidelines to consider when selecting your next trip into the magic world of print. For example: You should read the book that you hear two booksellers arguing about at the registers while you're browsing in a bookstore, or perhaps the book that you see someone on the train reading and trying to hide that they're laughing (or crying). You could read the book you find in your grandparents' house that's inscribed "To Phyllis with all my love" or the book you failed to read while enrolled in a high school English class. I often read one I find for cheap in a book exchange or that a friend loans me with his recommendations. Rarely do my eyes automatically scan expository text except when I am studying. Let the history guys untangle the love life of George Washington or best methods for planting corn in the desert. Give me a mystery or modern action adventure any day. Bottom line however: read, read, read.

Now, what about our reading of the Bible? What book, chapter, or verse have you read this week? As you crawled into bed, did you take a moment to scan your eyes over a psalm? Perhaps a friend has jogged your memory about the glorious words in Revelation 21:1–4 RSV: "Then I saw a new heaven and a new earth; for the first heaven and the first earth had passed away, and the sea was no more. And I saw the holy city, new Jerusalem, coming down out of heaven from God, prepared as a bride adorned for her husband; and I heard a great voice from the throne saying, Behold, the dwelling of God is with men. He will dwell with them, and they shall be his people, and God himself will be with them. He will wipe away every tear from their eyes, and death shall be no more, neither shall there be mourning or crying or pain anymore."

Or, if you are feeling down, sad, or discouraged, were you reminded by your spouse of James 1:2? "Count it all joy, my brethren, when you meet various trials, for you know that the testing of your faith produces steadfastness. And let steadfastness have its full effect, that you may be perfect and complete, lacking in nothing." Sharing passages of scripture with each other brings about encouragement and enhances friendships as well as provides "food" for the soul.

Okay, ready for the survey? Below are five situations where you might be able to recommend your favorite scripture, story, or passage to someone. Think about each. Maybe you will need to do a bit of research. (I had to.) Write down your answer. When you are finished, perhaps share the questions with a friend and then compare answers. You will grow as a lover of the Word.

1. A young fellow visits your home. He loves action and heroes but is restless. What story in the Bible might hold his attention? _____

2. A friend calls. A special person in his life has just been diagnosed with an incurable disease. What scripture would be helpful? _____

3. You have had a long, grueling day. Your nerves are frayed. Tempers are about to clash. Think of a Psalm to read that will help calm your soul. _____

4. The minister suggested the church members all give thanks for the wonderful blessings from God. Where might you turn for examples of thanksgiving blessings received? _____
5. You are invited to a baby shower for a first-time mother. Who in the Bible would be a great example of motherhood to share with this new mom-to-be? _____

Well, this school teacher just had to include a pop quiz. Think, research, enjoy, learn. Share with a friend.

What Are You Reading? Part II

Feedback from "Just for Fun Survey"

I INVITED READERS TO share passages of scripture that might be useful in helping others in their walk with Christ. Anticipating that perhaps no one would respond, I was thrilled as the first email arrived. A former minister answered almost immediately from his home in Salem, Illinois. The next response arrived from Taylorville, Illinois, followed by several Springfield readers.

One of the most exciting responses came from Ohio. A mother and her two children participated together as a family project. Sarah was our only reviewer who thought of Noah, the sailor, stranded on a boat for forty days and forty nights with his wife, kids, and a bunch of stinky animals as a great story to share with a restless young man. Andrew, the son, identified Ruth (although not a mom) as a great example of a first-time mom, as she was so faithful to her mother-in-law and stuck with her even when she was told to go off and get remarried.

Later in the week, we had a three-generation family participate: mother, daughter, and grandchild. It is thrilling to see families engaged with the Word and with each other in a spiritual way. I appreciated their involvement.

Certainly the Psalms have brought comfort to many. The most difficult scenario seemed to be ideas for the first-time mother. Regardless, I complimented everyone who took the time to share thoughts. One reader used online reference sources to help him recall ideas. Another person sent a message, thought some more, and then sent two additional emails. This writer rejoiced that so many readers took time to think about God's Word.

Situations and Sample Responses

1. **A young fellow visits your home. He loves action and heroes but is restless. What story in the Bible might hold his attention?** Most folks suggested the battle between David and Goliath, but Noah's ark adventure, Moses and his mountaintop experience acquiring the Ten Commandments, and Daniel taking a snooze in the lions' den were mentioned. David and his friend Jonathan and his life in general would also be good stories for this restless guy. And then we had Joshua and his battle at Jericho.

2. **A friend calls. A special person in his life has been diagnosed with an incurable disease. What scripture would be helpful?** "The righteous cry out, and the Lord hears them; he delivers them from all their troubles. The Lord is close to the brokenhearted" (Psalm 34:17–19), or from a different perspective, "I consider that our present sufferings are not worth comparing with the glory that will be revealed in us" (Romans 8:18). Take a moment to read Psalms 23, 30:5, 46:1, 61:1–2 and 5–8, 62:1–2; Isaiah 41:10; Jeremiah 29:11; 2 Corinthians 4:16; Philippians 4:6–7; Matthew 8:5–13.

3. **You have had a long, grueling day. Your nerves are frayed. Tempers are about to clash. Think of a Psalm to read that will help calm your soul.** Many Psalms were chosen, including 42:1–2, 5; 21; 23; 37; 46:1; 100; and 118. Also, "A fool gives full vent to his anger, but a wise man quietly holds it back" (Proverbs 29:11); "Come to me, all you who are weary and burdened, and I will give our rest" (Matthew 11:25–30); "Peace I leave you" (John 14:27); 1 Corinthians 13; and then a favorite: "But those who hope in the Lord will renew their strength. They will soar on wings like eagles; they will run and not grow weary, they will walk and not be faint" (Isaiah 40:31); James 1:19; and finally, "I can do everything through him who gives me strength" (Philippians 4:13).

4. **The minister suggested the church members all give thanks for the wonderful blessings from God. Where might you turn for**

examples of thanksgiving blessings received? Ephesians 1:3–12; Psalm 69:30; "Give thanks in all circumstances, for this is God's will for you in Christ Jesus" (1 Thessalonians 5:18); Psalm 95; 75:5; 118:1–4, 19–20; 138–139; 2 Peter 1:3–5; 1 Timothy 4:4; 1 Samuel 20; Philippians 4:4–7.

5. **You are invited to a baby shower for a first-time mother. Who in the Bible would be a great example of motherhood to share with this new mom-to-be?** Mother examples included Mary, the mother of Jesus; Eunice, the mother of Timothy; Hannah, Samuel's mom; Bathsheba, the mother of Solomon; and Jochebed, the mother who put her baby in a small boat and set him sailing (Moses); maybe even Eve, when you think of her being the first mom. It must have been tough for Eve, who had no previous examples from whom to learn proper baby caring techniques.

Perhaps you might want to invite your friends to think about these five situations. What a wonderful way for discussion with family or friends at dinner or sitting around a campfire

Gardening and Growth in Christ

What Is the Formula?

WALKING THE STREETS OF Athens, Greece, one day, this crazy looking garden stared me in the eyes—a pickup loaded with basil, daisies, onions, and other vegetation. Someone loved to garden or needed to make a living. What a unique way of marketing.

So what makes a green-thumbed gardener successful?

1. Commitment (Goal setting)

Success is preceded by clear, absolute focus on specific goals. The farmer wants healthy produce in order to satisfy customers.

2. Preparation

The soil must be prepared and fertilized for outstanding results. It takes work.

3. Seed Planting

Without healthy seeds, nothing, nada.

4. Care and Tending

The tough part: weeding, watering, and waiting for growth.

5. Harvesting

The joyful time when the radishes are red, raw, and ready for nibbling.

6. Sharing

Following harvest, a decision needs to be made whether to selfishly eat the overabundance of broccoli (which the kids hate anyway) or share with friends. Perhaps if one shares extra tomatoes, corn, or petunias with neighbors, some of their venison or pecan crop will land on your doorstep when hunting or nut season arrives.

Now, what about Christian growth? The Christian gardener should consider the same six elements. No, a green thumb is not required, but yes, planning is necessary. Growing in Christ necessitates being a gardener for the Lord.

1. **Commitment:** The Lord provides the charge. "If you love Me, you will obey what I command" (John 14:15). The command is, "Therefore go and make disciples of all nations" (Matthew 28:19). Christians must be committed to growing followers, not cabbages,

rosebuds, or dandelions. Which friend or acquaintance is not a believer? With whom could you share the Word?

2. **Preparation:** Two forms of preparation are required. The gardener must study the Word of God in order to present it clearly. Building friendships, being a role model of love, and sharing invitations to worship also are needed in preparing a new heart for hearing the Word.

3. **Seed Planting:** Be bold. Share a prayer. Drop off a little note to someone with a scripture. Invite others to a special program. That's seed planting. No seeds, no new birth.

4. **Care and Tending:** "They were continually devoting themselves to the apostles' teaching and to fellowship, to the breaking of bread and to prayer" (Acts 2:42). Care and feeding of Christians, especially newborns, includes reaching out and going out of our way to invite, pray, encourage, and model. Sometimes the plant almost dies, and extra tending is necessary. Accomplished gardeners keep a watchful eye on their garden of newly planted seeds. So must the Christian farmer.

5. **Harvest:** Seeing a friend or stranger start blooming as a new Christ follower is worth all of the tender care and feeding. Helping a struggling person over the weeds of life is well worth the effort. Let the harvest begin.

6. **Sharing:** Keep the circle going. Each one, win one, help one, pray for one. The seeds from your gardening products become the start of new growth the following year. So it is with new Christians. They, too, must immediately reach out to others. We cannot be selfish with our knowledge and love of God.

Share. What kind of gardener are you?

Three Castaways Rescued

Spelled "Help" with Palm Leaves

THREE FISHERMEN ABOARD A nineteen-foot skiff set off for a short sailing trip into the South Pacific. The weather grew rough, and a giant wave flipped the tiny craft over, tossing the guys into the salty, rough waters. Wearing life jackets, the trio swam in the dark to a small, deserted island almost two miles away. The island was Fanadik, several hundred miles north of Papua, New Guinea. For three days, they remained stranded, praying for rescue. Then, early on the third day, a crew aboard a US Navy plane zipping through the sky spotted the guys waving fluorescent orange life vests. They stood next to piles and piles of palm fronds on the sand that spelled H-E-L-P. Two hours later, a small boat arrived, picked them up, and took them to a hospital. Reportedly, the three were uninjured. I imagine, however, they were famished.

The Bible also shares some exciting water rescue stories, like "The Long Walk to the Sea, when the Children of Israel, after years of slavery, are finally ready to escape Egypt. The big evening arrives. Bags packed, cattle and sheep gathered up, and off they go only to be chased by Pharaoh's charging chariots (600 plus in number) right up to the shore of the Red Sea. Danger. "We will drown," they grumble. But no! Rescue is there. God causes an east wind to arise and blow all night long, causing the waters to divide. The seas part. The land is dry. Off the Israelites scurry to the other side, with nary a drop of water on their little toes (Exodus 14:13–31). "God to the Red Sea Rescue."

We read "Man Runs to the Sea: Jonah's Fish Boat." Jonah tries to skip out on preaching to the people in Nineveh as God requested. He dashes seaward and hops on a skiff headed toward Nineveh. A gigantic storm arrives, for which Jonah takes responsibility, knowing God is upset with him. Then, yo-ho-ho, the sailors pitch him into the water. And you know the rest of the story: A giant fish swallows him up. Jonah repents while incarcerated inside the "fish boat." Later, the fish spits him out onto the shore, thus saving the future preacher God lined up to call the Ninevites to repentance. All repent. What a rescue (Jonah 1–4).

Or what about our other pair of boat stories? Into his seaworthy creation, the 500-year-old man loads animals of all sorts plus family and waits for the water to come to him. God brings rain; for forty days and forty nights, Noah and family, plus stinky animals, rock and roll. But then, waters recede, and Noah's family is saved from the devastating worldwide flood. He thanks God for being present in his life (Genesis 5–10).

"Out of the Boat: Guy with Faith, Lost Faith, Regained Faith." While riding in a boat one evening, our friend Peter saw Jesus walking on the water. He boldly asked permission to walk on water also (Had faith). He climbed out of the boat but began to sink (Lost faith). Full of fear, Pete called out, "Lord, save me." (Jesus responded, "Be of good cheer," and extended His hand. Our fisherman reached out and took the hand and is saved (Faith regained) (Matthew 14:22–33).

Perhaps you, too, have almost drowned in deep waters of sorrow, pain, loneliness, worry, jealousy, or anger. Remember, and pray as David did when he faced many challenges including physical, political, and spiritual. "David sang to the Lord the words of this song when the Lord delivered him from the hand of all his enemies" and, "He reached down from on high and took hold of me; he drew me out of deep waters. He rescued me from my powerful enemy, from my foes, who were too strong for me" (2 Samuel 22:1, 17–18).

God has a rescue plan. Have faith.
Reach out and grab His hand. Be comforted.

"I Ain't No Scaredy Cat"

EVERY NOW AND THEN, a simple, heartwarming story passes my desk. This tale about a small puppy caused my heart to rejoice, at the behavior of the pooch as well as its owner, Terry Black. With his permission, I share this fun experience between a big guy who loves a little guy.

The Learning Experience

This is the story of a little dog named Ranger, who was afraid to enter a pedestrian tunnel that goes under the railroad tracks in Chatham. Ranger refused to go within fifteen feet of the entrance. When encouraged, he put his brakes on full. "No sir, I am not going in that scary place," he said with his body language.

So, his mentor, me, picked him up and walked into the gaping mouth of the tunnel. Since he was being held and really had no choice in the matter, Ranger remained calm while I carried him through the scary place.

When we emerged into the sunlight on the other side and I put him down on the concrete, he must have thought, *I'm glad that's over.*

Later, it was time to go back through the tunnel, so I could continue our walk back home. Surely he would be willing to make the trip on his own feet this time, but no, he wouldn't go. So once again, I picked him up, but this time, I stopped halfway through and put him down. We walked on with no problem at all. Entering the big black hole was the problem, but once inside, everything was okay.

The next day, we tried again, and Ranger walked right into the tunnel as though he had done it all his life. What do you know about that? I heard him whisper under his breath, "I ain't no scaredy cat."

Life is much like Ranger's experience. How often are we afraid? Afraid of spiders? Heights? Long, lonely nights? End-of-the-month bills? Giving speeches? Going to the home of your in-laws? Years ago, I was afraid to go into our basement to shovel coal into our furnace. The coal was stored back in a small, dark room. I would run down the stairs, open the furnace door, close my eyes, grab a shovel full of coal, and dump it into the furnace as quickly as possible. Up the stairs I would dash. Fear was gone for another morning, only to return twenty-four hours later. What do each of us need in distressing times like these? What about a friend?

Sharing our frightening challenges with a friend who cares can help, even if he or she just sits and listens. Our friend Jesus will pick us up or walk along by our side, no matter how rapidly our heart is pumping. The disciples were afraid as the storm rocked their boat, but the Master's voice calmed the waves. I should have prayed for peace as I dashed down to scoop up coal in the dark basement. Shame on me.

So we ain't going to be no scaredy cat. We are going to trust Jesus through rough and troubled times. Well, at least most of the times, but it would certainly help if God could just stick out an arm with flesh on it and grab us physically the next time we stand on some narrow, high rocky path of fear and uncertainty.

"Peace I leave with you; my peace I give you. I do not give to you as the world gives. Do not let your hearts be troubled and do not be afraid" (John 14:27).

"Fear not. I am with you. I am your God."

Passionate? "To Be or Not To Be," That Is the Question

**What does it mean to be passionate? What words or
ideas do you associate with passionate** people?
Obsessive? Affectionate? Fervent? Crazy? People demonstrate
passion for many things and in various forms.
For example:

PASSIONATE PEOPLE GIVE THEIR time and energies to their obsessions. Hours may be spent in the garage fine-tuning a favorite truck. Early mornings find others digging in the dirt, trimming bushes, or watering, almost forgetting to see the kids off to school. Committed photographers, artists, golfers, or mothers spend every waking moment engaged with their passion, sometimes even to the neglect of family or work. Some of us express strong opinions and feelings through loving or hurtful expressions or actions. Passion can be both rewarding and scary. Overall, however, I like passionate folks.

So what about Christians? Should we be passionate? Is fervency exemplary behavior or embarrassing and harmful? Will we drive folks away from worship and the church with expressions of strong feeling and emotion? Can true commitment and love only be demonstrated in a very vocal, expressive manner? Should we let our deep love for Christ and the church show through passionate outbursts, hugs, and energy, or should those expressions of joy be hidden deep in our heart? Lots of questions, but what do the scriptures say? Perhaps Paul might reward us with some insight: "But whatever was to my profit I now consider loss for the sake of Christ. What is more, I consider everything a loss compared to the surpassing greatness of knowing Christ Jesus my Lord, for whose sake I have lost all things. I consider them rubbish, that I may gain Christ and be found in him, not having a righteousness of my own that comes from the law, (Jewish) but that which is through faith in Christ—the righteousness that comes from God and is by faith" (Philippians 3:7–9).

What did Paul mean? We know that Saul/Paul left his life of fame and importance to follow Jesus. He suffered shipwrecks, beatings, and imprisonment because of his dedication to Christ. He was obsessed with telling the world about Christ. He gave up his former life, which engulfed his very being, to the degree that Saul held the garments of Stephen as he was stoned. No person could have been more passionate in a harmful way. But wonderful news. Christ redirected Saul's passion and energy. Saul became Paul, exhibiting incredible dedication and passion in responding to God's love.

Let's read the same passage in Philippians from a modern translation, The Message. Perhaps it better illustrates that obsessive, energetic, fervent spirit that possessed Paul. I encourage you to read the following passage at least three times. Then please take a moment and evaluate your own passion for Christ. Remember, it can be a quiet or exuberant demonstration as we witness for our Savior. Your love cannot be lukewarm and wishy-washy, or God will spit you out of his mouth (Revelation 3:6).

"Yes, all the things I once thought were so important are gone from my life. Compared to the high privilege of knowing Christ Jesus as my Master, firsthand, everything I once thought I had going for me is insignificant—dog dung. I've dumped it all in the trash so that I could embrace Christ and be embraced by him. I didn't want some petty, inferior brand of righteousness that comes from keeping a list of rules when I could get the robust kind that comes from trusting Christ—God's righteousness. I gave up all that inferior stuff so I could know Christ personally, experience his resurrection power, be a partner in his suffering, and go all the way with him to death itself. If there was any way to get in on the resurrection from the dead, I wanted to do it. I'm not saying that I have this all together, that I have it made. But I am well on my way, reaching out for Christ, who has so wondrously reached out for me" (Philippians 3:12 The Message).

**Yes! "To be" is the answer to our original question.
We must be passionate for Christ.**

God's Eye Is on This Little Creature

Guess Who Else He Is Watching?

THIS IS NO ORDINARY sparrow. This is a Portuguese sparrow found hopping, nibbling, and chirping with joy. As I crouched in the grass, focusing the camera, my mind shifted to the verse in Matthew 6:25–26: "Therefore I tell you, do not worry about your life, what you will eat or drink; or about your body what you will wear. Is not life more important than food, and the body more important than clothes Look at the birds of the air; they do not sow or reap or store away in barns, and yet your heavenly Father feeds them. Are you not more valuable than they?"

Sparrows during the Lord's lifetime were sold for less than a quarter (Matthew 10:29). So insignificant were these small creatures that if you bought four, the dealer often threw in one more for free. The poor who could not afford to sacrifice a sheep or goat would bring a sparrow to the temple as their offering. This simple, fluffy creation was watched by God and important to Him. "Not one of them is forgotten before God" (Luke 12:4–7). God provides for "the birds of the air" and even "clothes the grass of the field." How can we doubt that He cares for us, who are created in His own image? He knows our needs. He loves you. He watches me. We are His beloved. So stop worrying. Yes, that is easier said than done, but we must learn to trust.

God, however, does not prevent evil, sorrow, or pain from happening. Bad things happen. God does not prevent the sparrow from falling, but He watches over our feathered friend, even as the predator hunts him. So it is with us, His human children. He is watching over us as Satan tempts us or sends trials our way. He is still by our side when we make stupid decisions and cause harm to ourselves or our families. He cares. Sometimes, He just does not overtly respond as swiftly as we humans might wish.

Paul admonishes the Christians in Philippi to "Rejoice in the Lord always. I will say it again: Rejoice! Let your gentleness be evident to all. The Lord is near. Do not be anxious about anything, but in everything, by prayer and petition, with thanksgiving, present your requests to God. And the peace of God, which transcends all understanding, will guard your hearts and minds in Christ Jesus" (Philippians 4:4–7). Now isn't that a splendid challenge? Pray, petitioning for support, help, comfort, health, family, the lost, but pray with thanksgiving. Yes, it is hard to pray and be thankful when pain reaches every cell in your body, or your best friend has just passed away, or your child is addicted to drugs. But Paul says that it is our responsibility as a Christian to rejoice, to pray, to give thanks. Then we remember that Jesus knows when sparrows fall and cares about them. Certainly, He is even more caring about us, His children. So today, remember to rejoice and pray. Pray for healing, faith, and understanding for others.

Let the world know you are a Christian just by watching the smile on your face and the peace in your heart. His eye is on

Y

O

U

How Long Is a Minute?

RECENTLY WHILE DRIVING, I found my mind grumbling at the length of the stoplight. How could the city possibly set the timing so slow? Then to top it off, the driver in front hesitated at least four seconds before accelerating. My mind shouted out, "Hurry, mister; I need to keep moving." I probably was delayed fifteen and a half seconds at the most, but my negative attitude followed me for several blocks. To make it worse, I really wasn't even late for an appointment—just impatient.

As I continued on my travels, I began to analyze my behavior. Why was a l-o-n-g stoplight upsetting? Why did I mentally scream at the overly cautious driver ahead of me? Did a minute delay really make any difference? And then the question popped into my gray-covered head: how long really is a minute? It depends.

It depends on what you are doing. If being held under water by a giant sea creature, a minute is an eternity. If, however, you are drifting slowly down a lazy river atop an inner tube surrounded by friends and warm sunlight, a minute is but a moment. You crave multiple minutes of bliss. Fleeing a forty-story building in flames with lungs filled with smoke, you hope a minute extends until you exit into fresh air. Or perhaps a loved one has tumbled off an ocean liner into the raging sea. Your heart pleads for an extended minute. Time cannot go slowly enough as you or others leap overboard to assist in a rescue. Yes, at times, we want minutes to move swiftly, and in other situations, we hope that the clock stops running.

I am reminded of Abraham when commanded by God to sacrifice his only son. As he prepares for the journey to fulfill God's command, what would he be thinking? Selecting the firewood, packing a few belongings, and informing Sarah, his wife, of his mission, he sets off with an aching heart. Trudging up the hill accompanied by son, two servants, and a donkey, surely his mind must have sought ways to extend minutes—to think of ways to stop time. Perhaps he even tried to delay the journey, maybe by taking a rock out of his sandal or stopping to count the butterflies on a branch or ... But now the time has come to offer the sacrifice—Isaac—his longed-for son. *How can I do this?* The knife is raised. It will take not a minute, not even ten seconds to lower the blade. His heart is breaking, but because he trusts and loves the Lord, he will follow His commands. His final words to Isaac are, "The Lord will provide the lamb." Then, just as the knife is ready to slay his son, the angel of the Lord calls out, "Abraham! Abraham! Do not lay a hand on the boy. Do not do anything to him. Now I know that you fear God, because you have not withheld from me your son, your only son" (Genesis 22:1–19).

Just think how long those seconds would seem while Abraham's arm descended toward the throat of the boy. He would be praying for delay, the very opposite of your impatient author at the stoplight. Imagine the change in his facial expressions, the slowing of the beating heart, the immense relief, the joy in that change of plans. He reaches into the thicket, pulls out the ram the Lord provided, and makes the new sacrifice.

So, what might we learn from these musings on minutes? Time is really irrelevant to the Lord. A day may be like a thousand years on God's clock. We must learn to adapt to His timeframe. Trust is the key word. When events are not going as you wish them, pray for understanding and patience. That last word is almost impossible for me to greet with friendliness. Hurry is the name of my game, just not the name of God's plan. He answers prayers, sometimes in a minute, other times more like an eternity. We want instantaneous healing. We pray for quick solutions to rocky relationships. Some even pray for God to take them to eternity—now—and He replies, "You do not know the day or the hour" (Matthew 25:13). We have to learn to wait.

> I guess honking at the Lord will not cause
> Him to move more swiftly.
> Be patient.
> Remember, though, He is coming again.

"We Are Not Called to Ride on a Cruise Ship but on a Battleship"

IN HIS THOUGHT-PROVOKING SERMON Sunday, December 27, 2015, Matt McClane, youth minister at South Side Christian Church in Springfield, Illinois, made that statement. My ears perked up, and my mind sailed through scriptures and my life, charting out passages for application. Never had I made this comparison. New and fresh ideas absolutely are exhilarating, even for someone eight decades old. The application related to his theme of *Fight the Chaos in our Lives*. Very appropriate, I thought, but to what else might this analogy apply?

The mental and Google search began. To what battles has the Lord called us? Yes, of course, we are to be soldiers of the cross. Actually, in days long gone, it was okay to sing the song "Onward, Christian Soldiers." Off we journeyed to fight the war against sin. Sadly, today, our song leaders often ignore such hymns. Allegedly, it is politically incorrect to share with folks outside of Christ that we are warriors against Satan and his host. But yes, we need to hop into the tar-and-pitch-covered basket with Moses, sail among the reeds, and grow into a real leader standing up to the Pharaohs of today. Are you ready to lead your family and friends through the Red Sea of today's trials and challenges? Good. You are ready for battleship duty.

The inventory of scripture continued, and I realized we are each in a spiritual battle, a battle against sin in our own lives. We cruise along comfortably in our dream-ship vacation. Simultaneously, Satan sends out tantalizing opportunities for us to forget our goal to be Christlike. Satan snags us. We have failed to don our armor, as found in Ephesians 6:10–20. We pray spasmodically or in a rote manner. Perhaps we have forgotten to put on the breastplate of righteousness. Am I wearing feet shod with knowledge of peace after studying His Word? Do we have that shield of faith gripped tightly in our fist, or are we swaying in the wind with every little challenge to our faith? The Lord's battleship must have appropriately clad followers, so reread Ephesians 6.

In 1 Peter 5:8, (RSV), we are reminded to "Be sober, be watchful; Your adversary the devil prowls around like a roaring lion, seeking someone to devour." Paul shares with the youthful Timothy a wonderful testimony about his own life battling the trials and tribulations of existence: "I have fought the good fight. I have finished the race. I have kept the faith" (2 Timothy 4:7). Join hands with fellow Christians in times of fear. Pray together for healing or wisdom. Ask a fellow warrior to listen when you are tempted to embarrass the Lord with your actions or thoughts. Remember that, figuratively, Jesus is in your boat to guide and counsel. He joined the disciples as they needed their faith strengthened when the storms were tossing the boat about. He will not forget you either (John 6:21).

Every ship has life-saving equipment like safety rings. So also does our ship with Christ as the captain. Are you prepared to let the Holy Spirit work through you to truly help a friend, neighbor, or stranger fight off a problem? Check your spiritual readiness. How would you help an individual experiencing one of the following situations?

A. Loss of a spouse and a child in less than two weeks' time.
B. A shut-in experiencing tremendous pain and loneliness.
C. A friend who is puzzled over the meaning of a passage of scripture.
D. A parent worried about a child's inappropriate decisions relating to sexual abstinence.

E. A Christian worker facing tremendous financial challenges in his or her personal life or organization.

Warriors are ready. "Take your share of suffering as a good soldier of Christ Jesus" (2 Timothy 2:3 RSV).

No, we are not soldiers with real swords and shields of steel, but we are to fight the battle with the sword of the Scripture. Therefore, continue to arm yourself with tremendous study of the Bible so you will be a "ready warrior," not a "cruise snoozer."

"All scripture is God breathed and is useful for teaching, rebuking, correcting, and training in righteousness" (2 Timothy 3:26).

Baby Koala Clings to His Mom while She Undergoes Surgery

LIZZY, THE KOALA, WAS taken to a wildlife hospital in an Australian zoo, with her son holding onto her side. She had been hit by a car. Her little boy, Phantom, only six months old, was luckily unharmed but refused to leave his mother. Lizzy suffered a collapsed lung that required emergency surgery. Phantom continued to hold on and would not leave her, even during the operation. Lizzy survived and recovered with Phantom by her side. This amazing display of a son's love for his mother is heartwarming.

Daily, we hear other stories of parental sacrifice and love for their offspring. Some mothers resist the meaty chicken parts and nibble away on a wing so their children may indulge. Parents work long hours, often two jobs, to provide meals, school supplies, homes, clothing, and even a few luxuries for their children. Only once did I see my mom ever buy herself a new coat, and that was after both of her children were off to college. Parents work night shifts in order to be at home when the children are awake, but in exchange, they sacrifice their own sleep.

Dads and moms often scold and discipline their kids, resulting in misunderstandings by the children. Johnny and Melissa assume their parents hate them, and in turn, they become angry, snarly, or silent just to spite their parents. Why did the adults discipline the kids? They loved and cared and wanted only the best for each of their offspring.

We also hear of children displaying overt love for their moms or dads. Kids have taken jobs to help the family budget. During the drought in Egypt, Joseph took care of his father and brothers, even though his brothers had betrayed him. Jesus asked ~~Peter~~ John to care for his mom as He hung on the cross. Older youth and adults spend hours at nursing homes or other care centers with aging parents. Why? Because they love.

We, too, have a Parent Who cares for us. In fact, He even gave His Son for you and me. His arms are willing to hold us in times of stress and doubt, but we need to cling to Him. Close is good when we care. We must not drift away through neglect, busy schedules, selfish priorities, or tiredness.

God, our Father, is full of love, but we have to be near enough to reach out. Yes, sometimes He may even discipline us, but only because He loves us. Don't become like the snarly kid, pouting and running away like the prodigal son. Take your medicine and double your efforts to please Dad. Give your all. Pray more. Share continually with others the message of God's love. Pass His love on through service and caring for others.

Many of His children need encouragement, flowers, friendship, or just your time demonstrating you care. Remember who your neighbor is. Love them as you love yourself or your own family. They might even enjoy a couple of chocolate bonbons or an offer of a cup of tea around the kitchen table.

Let love shine forth.
Hang on tight to the Lord.

Time for Thanksgiving

Life Is Great

How blessed we are as Christians, so let's give thanks today:
"Give thanks to the Lord, for he is good; his love
endures forever" (1 Chronicles 16:34).

"In that day you will say, 'Give thanks to the Lord, call on
his name; make known among the nations what he has done,
and proclaim that his name is exalted'" (Isaiah 12:4).

"For this reason, ever since I heard about your faith in the Lord Jesus and your love for all the saints, I have not stopped giving thanks for you, remembering you in my prayers" (Ephesians 1:15–16).

"Give thanks in all circumstances, for this is God's will for you in Christ Jesus" (1 Thessalonians 5:18).

"The Lord is my strength and my shield; my heart trusts in him, and I am helped. My heart leaps for joy and I will give thanks to him in song" (Psalm 28:7).

Thanks for an Another Answer to a Bold, Believing Prayer

APPROXIMATELY THREE YEARS AGO, a team of dedicated friends of Lake Springfield Christian Assembly (LSCA) accepted the challenge of raising over a million dollars to provide funds for the completion of Eagle Lodge. With the help of hundreds of loyal campers and Christians, bills were paid as the building slowly took shape. Volunteers helped with many tasks, reducing the actual dollars necessary. A gigantic garage sale and other events provided dollars. We were on our way with giant amounts of enthusiasm.

But as the weeks passed, revenue slowed down. A small loan was taken out. Discouragement began to creep into the hearts of our volunteers and committee. But God helped us see a light at the end of the long tunnel. Dr. Don Green, president of Lincoln Christian University (LCU), sent a letter to friends of the university. He requested that we begin to pray bold, believing, united, constant, Kingdom-centered, specific prayers for LCU. The committee took his request and applied it to our campaign at camp.

One example. Gravel was needed for the new drive so folks would not get stuck in the mud. The estimate for eight hundred tons of rock came in at $28,000. Kerma and Gale, camp managers, looked at the estimate and thought, *No way. We just don't have the money.* Kerma walked to the office, praying, "God, we need rock." Opening the phone book, she randomly called the number of a vendor. After identifying herself with LSCA and explaining what she needed, there was a pause.

The voice asked, "Is this where Gale works?"

"Yes," Kerma responded.

The voice continued, "I knew him years ago at church. Let me see what I can do." After waiting a few moments, the voice came back. The bill would be $10,000, not the $28,000 from the first bid. Bold, believing, answered prayer. Renewed energy, and on we moved.

Well, friends, we had a second example of answered prayer. A few months later, $150,000 remained for the final payment of the loan. Frankly, by this time, my faith had diminished to a mere shadow on a dark day. Ideas for raising the final dollars were absent. Names of friends to contact had long been exhausted. Nighttime often was filled with wakefulness as discouragement filled my heart. We had a job to do (raise $150,000), with absolutely no idea what to do next. We had prayed specifically for a major donor who might be able to provide $100,000. Our prayers were sincere and bold. Oh, me of little faith. I gave up.

About a week later, I received a call from Kerma. She had just been notified a gift for Eagle Lodge was coming. It was a significant gift. As she told me the amount, I almost cried. A friend of camp was selling some stock, and the amount of the gift would be about $148,000. Yes, just the amount needed, along with what we had in the bank, to finish off the lodge.

Am I thankful today? You bet I am.
Am I a more sincere believer of bold, believing prayer?
Absolutely.

The Perfect Church

"SO MY DREAM CHURCH would include leather La-Z-Boys in the sanctuary. They would automatically recline for the sermon. Of course, even lounging on a La-Z-Boy is no fun if you're hungry. Most churches provide subpar coffee with a few stale snacks. Not in my dream church. We'd have a full breakfast buffet with one of those guys in a white chef hat cooking made-to-order omelets. To me, nothing says Christian community quite like a fresh southwest omelet with fresh-squeezed orange juice and a side of bacon." These interesting thoughts are the words of Brett McCracken from his book, *Uncomfortable: The Awkward and Essential Challenge of Christian Community.*

Perhaps each of us has envisioned the perfect church. Reflecting on McCracken's comments, however, I was struck with the emphasis on a building and amenities dealing with feeling good and comfortable. The author was attempting to capture creature comforts within the walls of a facility. Certainly, we each appreciate various styles of architecture, lounges for people to gather, pews with comfy cushions, or perhaps soft carpet and ample restroom facilities. Structures are varied; many located in recycled facilities formerly a theater, big-box store, or garage, which appeals to many of the younger generation. But having acknowledged this, we must remember what the church really is.

Each of us has been guilty of saying, "I'm going to church" or "over to the church." What we really mean, however, is I am going to the building where the church meets. The building is not the church. We, the believers in Christ, are the church—the Body of Christ. The familiar admonition by Paul to the Ephesians helps define the church: "Husbands, love your wives, just as Christ loved the church and gave himself up for her, to make her holy, cleansing her by the washing with water through the word, and to present her to himself as a radiant church, without stain or wrinkle or any other blemish, but holy and blameless" (Ephesians 5:25–27). Certainly, Paul was not suggesting that Christ loved a building, died for a structure, or plans to present a church that is a pile of bricks and mortar in the end that is without blemish. We, the recipients of His love and washed by His blood, compose the church. We will be blemish free.

Perhaps we need to refresh our memories regarding what makes up the church by reading Ephesians 2:19–20: "You are no longer foreigners and aliens, but fellow citizens with God's people and members of God's household, built on the foundation of the apostles and prophets, with Christ Jesus himself as the chief cornerstone." Again, we see the analogy to a physical building with a cornerstone, but what is that cornerstone? None other than Christ Himself. A physical structure does not have Christ as a cornerstone. Generally, the building cornerstone is a block of concrete or marble upon which words have been inscribed. Paul is talking about a building composed of washed-by-the-blood humans with lumps, bumps, imperfections, pimples, and varied talents and personalities. You, my dear reader, are a brick in Christ's church.

Now, if that is true, we have a problem. Ugh! He desires a perfect church, a group of bricks (Christians) without spot or blemish. What a challenge. In any one day, I seem to manage to blemish my brick multiple times with unloving thoughts, careless words, selfish acts, or multiple other inappropriate activities. Do we become so concerned about appearances or about feeling good and comfortable ourselves that we lose track of to whom the church belongs? It is His church. We belong to Him. He shed His blood for us. It is a priceless, awesome treasure worth selling all and returning it to the owner: Christ. We are just stewards of His riches. This includes our physical bodies as well as our talents, wealth, and energy. Remember, Paul said, "I no longer live, but Christ lives in me" (Galatians 2:20). The body of believers is urged to gather and worship, expressing their love weekly, but then the church moves out to serve.

Christ's church is not static. The body moves around. You are a part of the body of Christ, and therefore, as you dash through home, town, work venue, or ball diamond, part of Christ is present. Our goal is to be as Christlike as possible. Through His grace, we seek forgiveness for our daily blemishes. Then, "Let your light shine before men, that they may see your good deeds and praise your Father in heaven" (Matthew 5:16).

So, up out of the La-Z-Boys and into the world as servants of Christ. With blemishes, of course.

Endangered Species: Sea Turtles and?

A TURNAROUND IS HAPPENING in Florida. In 2016, record-breaking numbers of sea turtles nested in Florida. In early September, 20,376 loggerheads nested at Archie Carr National Wildlife Refuge. This surpassed previous highs of 2012 by five hundred. Other nesting spots have also recorded record numbers of nests but still far below historical levels. The Endangered Species Act has helped accelerate the turnaround. Manatees and gray wolves also experience declining numbers. Friends of wildlife are concerned. What will disappear next? The tiny land turtle found in Hwange Park, Africa? Can the wolves be saved? What action do lovers of wildlife need to initiate?

Another disturbing headline grabs my eyes and causes even more distress: "After Christians and Muslims, 'No Religion' is the World's Third-Largest Religious Group." Reuters reported this news in 2010. CNN reporter Daniel Burke's headline from the Pew Research Center also caught my attention: "Millennials Leaving Church in Droves, Study

Finds" (May 14, 2015). The survey of thirty-five thousand American adults shows the Christian percentage of the population dropping to 70.6 percent, down from 78.4 percent in 2007. More than one-third of millennials now say they are unaffiliated with any faith. Perhaps this 2013 headline will also cause you to be concerned: "Religion among Americans Hits Low Point, as More People Say They Have No Religious Affiliation."

So the question is, are Christians an endangered species? Surveys indicate that the number of folks who do not consider themselves part of an organized religion has increased dramatically. Research suggests that men are more likely than women to claim they have no religion (24 percent compared to 16 percent). African Americans and Mexican Americans are more likely to associate themselves with a religion than whites.

What is happening? What caused this change in values and religious identification? Why have 30 percent of millennials dropped even nominal identification with any religion? Has "busy-busy-busy" invaded their lives? Perhaps technology worship replaced worship of God. Should parents and grandparents accept responsibility for this movement away from God's Kingdom? Have we failed to provide sufficient modeling of a Christlike spirit and an attitude of love and service? What about youth and young adult church leaders? Have they replaced in-depth study of the scriptures with social and behavioral talk time? Could it be that the twenty-plus-year-old has no solid scriptural knowledge and so drifts away?

One writer has suggested that young Christians seemed bored by church. A study by Greg Jones from Duke University found that nearly 70 percent of full-time youth ministers have no theological education. Perhaps these youth leaders lack the skills necessary to biblically connect with the adults of tomorrow. Is boredom or lack of understanding of the need to participate, help, share, and love others turning our youth away from God? If yes, we need to take action now.

What Can You Do?

- Pray that young lives will be reached for Christ. Be specific with actual names of folks.

- Make a personal connection with at least two young people (sixteen to twenty-four age range). Invite them to dinner, take a walk together, or ask them to help rake your leaves and then feed them while sharing Christian love. Friendships develop into new relationships. Relationships build long-term Christian commitments. Commitments build church leaders.
- Be creative, but find that high school/college graduate (millennial) and figure out how to talk, work, play, enjoy, and care together. Through those experiences, we may keep fewer young people from turning their back on the Lord.

Let's reverse the decline of commitment to the Lord from our youth and adults, just like the sea turtle turnaround.

Endangered or Just Threatened? (Part II)

BOTTLENOSE DOLPHINS ARE STILL in deep water. In 2010, petroleum spills devastated one of our most popular marine mammals. The bottlenose is a social animal and generally found in a group of two to fifteen or in herds of up to one hundred. They enjoy hunting together.

The waters off the islands of Hawaii and the coasts of Japan, Australia, California, Mexico, Chile, and other warm-water areas are perfect habitats for these creatures. These areas are also often spots for net fishing. Annually, approximately five thousand dolphins get entrapped in the fishing gear. Even though fishermen frequently release them, the dolphins have been damaged sufficiently to be unable to live. Chemical spills and other pollutants challenge their environment. Measures need to be taken now to save these graceful mammals.

So why mention this today? Perhaps the church also has endangered or threatened elements. Reflecting on the church nationwide, three concerns flash before my eyes: compassion, community, and commitment.

Compassion: Caring for one another. The church in Philippi sent Epaphroditus to minister to Paul while in prison. It probably took him over a month by ship to get to Caesarea from Philippi. The journey would have been challenging and expensive. Paul tells us that Epaphroditus became so ill on the way that he almost died. But the Christians were concerned about Paul's health, so he made the sacrifice. We are told to become like little children, children who care. Have we become so busy and focused on our own families and personal interests that we are failing to reach out to the poor, hurting, grieving, ethnically or socially different, or friendless? Is compassion just a word in the dictionary and not displayed through our deeds?

Community: Seventy percent of young adults drop out of church. One out of five church dropouts indicated that they had no meaningful relationship with other members of the church. Paul in his letter to the Philippians calls himself a servant of Christ. He wrote his letter to "friends" in the church. What happened to opportunities for sharing, eating, serving, talking, or playing together? Members of the early church broke bread together. Yes, we are each different with uncommon interests, but surely we can take time to reach out to the stranger in our midst with a smile and some conversation. Perhaps you can have a sandwich after church with that visitor sitting alone in your pew. Friends reach out and stay connected to each other. Chess games, picnics, bike hikes, or quilting days build relationships with others. Are we only making community with those just like ourselves? Are we shunning folks who are different—different color, social standing, or education? Could this be an endangered element in the church of today? You decide.

Commitment: Christianity is a 24/7, lifetime commitment. We belong to Christ every day of our lives—not just for sixty minutes each Sunday. This description by Wilbur Rees illustrates my concern: "Dear God. I would please like to buy three dollars worth of you. Not enough to explode my soul or disturb my sleep, but just enough to equal a cup of lukewarm milk or a snooze in the sunshine. I want a pound of the Eternal in a paper sack. I would like to buy three dollars worth of God, please." We want a moderate Christ who makes few demands. Time, energy, tears, and hugs are for someone else, a diminishing someone else.

Many of you reading this are in the minority. You do care. You do shed tears for others. Your heart and energy work full time for the Kingdom. Our challenge now is how do we ignite the "serve-others" spark in our neighbors? Plant seeds to help turned-off folks begin to deeply care for others. Share these thoughts with at least one other person this week.

Pray for increase in compassion, community, and commitment.
Burn out for Christ.
Do not let Christianity become history.

Strange Bundles Arrive with New Parcel Post Service

MORE THAN ONE HUNDRED years ago, our US Post Office decided to start shipping large packages through the mail. This new service was especially helpful to residents in rural communities. Suddenly, millions of folks had access to all types of goods and services. But as is often true with new experiments, there was an unintended consequence. US Postal Service historian Jenny Lynch shares a wonderful tale.

Allegedly, some parents decided to ship their children through the mail, according to Lynch (smithsonianmag. com/smart-news/ brief-history-children-sent-through-mail). Shortly after Parcel Post began, an Ohio couple named Jesse and Mathilda Beagle "mailed" their eight-month-old son, James, to his grandmother, who lived just a few miles away in Batavia.  Evidently, James was just shy of the eleven-pound weight limit for a package sent via Parcel Post. The delivery cost his parents only fifteen cents in postage (they did, however, insure him for fifty dollars). This unique story captured the headlines of several newspapers of the day, and so apparently other parents replicated the travel service.

When we approach the Christmas season, I am reminded of another parent who shipped His Son off to a faraway land. This Son was living with His Father from the beginning of time, but Dad sent a gift to us. "For God so loved the world that he gave his one and only son, that whoever believes in him shall not perish but have eternal life" (John 3:16). People were just as amazed at the arrival of Jesus as the grandmother of James was when the squirmy little one popped up in her mailbox that evening in 1913. In fact, Wise Men came from afar to worship this promised King of the Jews. Even King Herod wanted to find this new bundle of babyhood, but not for celebration. Today, we still remember the newborn Child and celebrate His birth, death, and ultimate resurrection. What a package sent to you and me.

The postage for the child was cheaper than a train ticket. No wonder the parents used their creative powers to think of this clever delivery system. Our package of the Christ Child is a free gift. "For the wages of sin is death, but the gift of God is eternal life in Christ Jesus our Lord" (Romans 6:23). Ultimately, however, it cost the Father the life of His Son. Think of the pain in the Father's heart as well as the tears of grief by Mary, the earthly delivery system. No parent wants to bury a child. The heavy price included separation from His mother, excruciating personal pain through death, loss, and loneliness by His disciples. Nothing cheap about this shipment from God to us by those close to Jesus.

Finally, on June 14, 1913, several newspapers including the *Washington Post*, the *New York Times*, and the *Los Angeles Times* ran stories stating that the postmaster had officially decreed that children could no longer be sent through the mail. We, too, will never experience another shipment of a Savior sent for our salvation. God sent only one official package, labeled "Immanuel," which means "God with us" (Matthew 1:23). How blessed we are. Yes, we could even say this is a Flag Day worthy of our celebration.

Some might hint that mailing children demonstrated incompetence or negligence by the parents. Lynch, however, suggests that this action suggested how much mail carriers were trusted by the folks in the early twentieth century. How true also for Christ followers today. We trust our delivery service implicitly. God keeps His promises. In fact, He even promised us a second gift, mentioned by Peter in Acts 2:38: "Repent and be baptized, every one of you, in the name of Jesus Christ for the forgiveness of your sins. And you will receive the gift of the Holy Spirit." This promise continues even to today.

Celebrate and share this package today with a friend.

Four in Ten Adult Americans Still Sleep with Teddy

Are You One of Those Four in Ten? Why Would Adults Still Cuddle These Furry Friends?

BUILD-A-BEAR WORKSHOP RECENTLY CONDUCTED a survey of over two thousand folks, resulting in amazing findings. Adults apparently retain a love for their tiny cub friend (or other stuffed animal) left over from childhood; 56 percent of those polled said that their little creature was at least two decades old, and 72 percent wanted to keep their stuffed animal forever.

The researchers discovered that adults found these animal friends brought them comfort or encouraged them to think of the gift-giver. Folks seemed to feel teddy bears provided a sense of security, especially as they transitioned from childhood to young adult responsibilities. Comfort versus feelings of uncertainty became a priority. Best Mattress Brand also conducted a survey and found a higher number of millennials take these comfy toys to bed, more than any other generation studied.

Each of us has experienced stress and anxiety, both as children and as adults. We all seek peace, security, and comfort. The future holds moments of wonder, doubt, and a bit of fear, even for Christians. Yes, we are confident in our final abode with the Lamb of God, but getting there from wheelchair, comfort care, or family care can make our pulse escalate. How will we feel? Will our money last as long as the Lord has us last? What about friends and family left behind; will they be okay? We trust God, but being imperfect humans, our minds get sidetracked with uncertainty, pain, and love for others. These moments of panic or dread do, indeed, disturb our snoozing. Even counting sheep or saying the alphabet backwards fails to swoop us into dreamland.

What about Christians? Do we need a bear friend? Maybe, but more importantly, we need the arms of the loving Lord to surround us with joy, confidence, faith, and peace of mind. We have an assurance that He will be with us until the time we join Him in our heavenly home. One reason we hug a cub is the need for a sense of security or a feeling of love.

Paul shares a wonderful promise for Christians that we need to harbor in our hearts: "For I am convinced that neither death or life, neither angels or demons, neither the present nor the future, nor any powers, neither height nor depth, nor anything else in all creation, will be able to separate us from the love of God that is in Christ Jesus our Lord" (Romans 8:38–39). Perhaps when feelings of detachment, lonesomeness, or separation overcome us, we may mumble in our heads, "Does God really care about insignificant me?" Paul addresses this issue as he writes to Christians in Ephesus. He prays that God will give them the spirit of wisdom and revelation so that they will know Him better. Paul continues praying that "the eyes of your heart may be enlightened in order that you may know the hope to which he has called you, the riches of his glorious inheritance in the saints, and his incomparably great power for us who believe" (Ephesians 1:18-19)

God knows all our secrets, worries, and moments of emptiness. The Holy Spirit was sent by God to comfort us. We are protected from our enemies of self-condemnation, feelings of unworthiness, and anger if we just acknowledge the Spirit within us. We are secure in Christ Jesus if we have accepted His grace and acknowledged our sin. But we must trust and believe. David in Psalm 57:1–3 (The Message) says, "Be good to me, God— and now! I've run to you for dear life. I'm hiding out under your wings until the hurricane blows over. I call out to High God, the God who holds me together. He sends orders from heaven and saves me, he humiliates those who kick me around. God delivers generous love, he makes good on His Word." Paul has words of encouragement in Ephesians 1:12. Open the Word and read.

So, cuddle the floppy-eared bunny if you like, but remember prayers of thanksgiving to our God of love. Pray that you will trust Him. Cry out in pain and fear, but then listen. Listen to His quiet words:

"Peace I leave with you, my peace I give to you. I do not give to you as the world gives. Do not let your hearts be troubled and do not be afraid" (John 14:27).

Remember the Gift-Giver and His gift of eternal life with Him.

(The bear pictured is eighty-three years old, given to this writer on her arrival in this world. "Bear" traveled from coast to coast with me as a child and today is curled up on my dresser. My dad's brother, Uncle Justin, brought it to a Portland, Oregon, hospital on September 8, 1935. If you were to observe Bear up close, you would find the back of one ear has been shaved. Dad shaved, so I practiced on Bear.)

A Wreck! Auto, Yes! Your Life?

A WHILE BACK, I captured this image while driving down Eleventh Street in Springfield. Flashing red lights, reduced lane of traffic, and folks huddled around the car quickly drew my attention. Swooping up my cell phone on the seat, I clicked to capture the crumbling scene. Bingo! Yes, I know I probably should have focused on driving, not on photography.

Liquid poured from the vehicle. Crumpled, silver fenders, broken bumper, crushed interior—wow. Repairs will require more than just a push through the automatic car wash. Concerned folks stood by the door, talking with the driver seated inside. My guess is that this person was a bit shaken up. Hopefully, no serious injuries occurred.

As I drove through the intersection, my mind thought about the comparison of our lives to this auto. Each of us has also experienced bumps and bruises as we drive through life. Family conflicts. Impatience resulting in wrong decisions or angry words. Bad choices with careers, soulmates, eating habits, recreational activities, or health and wellness decisions, or attitudes needing adjustments. Have any of you experienced difficulties in those areas? Of course you have. Each of us has experienced some life disaster because we all sin or make goofy choices. We damage our lives, health, and influence for Christ or relationships with others. We are wrecks (or at least have some serious bumps).

Although the car wash will not repair our crumped disaster, talented auto body repair shops can perform miracles if the owner pays the asking price. What about our wrecked lives? Is there a proper repair shop? Yes, indeed. Let's think about that.

A few comparisons come to mind when I view the disaster of the silver bomb.

1. Window washer fluid appeared on the road. That liquid becomes crucial during certain times while driving. Clear vision is essential to safety. Water is also important in the life of a Christian. Participating in water baptism, we receive forgiveness as we access Christ's blood sacrifice on the cross for each of us. His sacrifice cleansed us and freed us from sin, a necessity for eventual life safety (Acts 2:38, 1 John 1:7). We also need clear vision as we watch the King of Kings and anticipate sharing life with Him.

2. The exterior protective covering of the auto was crumpled and ugly. We are reminded by Paul in Ephesians 6 about the armor of God. Here he describes what Christians need to do to protect their souls, not their physical bodies. We need to fill our lives with truth, righteousness, peace, faith, and acceptance of Jesus as our Savior, and then add knowledge of the Word of God. Adding prayer to our lives, we help protect ourselves, not from bugs and rain, as the silver metal does for the auto driver, but from the darts of Satan and everyday life.

3. Glancing again at the photo, it appears that the engine was somewhat smashed. Without an engine, this beautiful auto is virtually useless. As a Christian, we receive the gift of the Holy Spirit into our lives. His presence in our minds and hearts keeps our Christian lives in gear. God sent the Holy Spirit to be our Helper, Comforter, and Guide (John 14:16). In addition, the Spirit is the engine that helps us produce His fruit in our lives: love,

joy, peace, patience, kindness, goodness, faithfulness, gentleness, and self-control (Galatians 5:22–23). Minus these nine attributes, our lives become as damaged as this hunk of metal. We jolly well better repair our peace, joy, and kindness actions, or we are crushed merchandise. Perhaps we need to make a mental checklist of damaged fruit in our daily behaviors. Kindness and joy fill my heart with regularity, but oh me, I truly need a fresh supply of patience.

Are you ready to take an inventory of your spiritual life?
Which fruit of the spirit needs the most repair in your
behavior with friends, family, and the Lord?
Think about it.
Then dash to Christ's auto-repair shop and pray for restoration.

Might in the Mite of the Mature

What good is a penny?

NOT MUCH, YOU SAY? Penny candy is history. Hardly anyone remembers the penny postcard, which now costs forty-three cents. Penny loafers are no more. The government would love to stop minting the lonely cent. The penny is in trouble. But what does Jesus think about the penny? One day while in the temple, He calls the twelve over, and the teacher teaches (see Mark 12:38–44 and Luke 21:1–4). "Guys! Have you noticed those rich fellows dropping in big amounts in the offering box? Wow, how wonderful to have those important worshippers at our temple. The temple leaders will be able to pay the bills. Did you also notice the widow in her simple garments as she dropped in a couple of copper coins? What thoughts went through your mind when you saw her? Perhaps, you mumbled, 'Wish she would get out of the way so the rich can pour in their giant gifts?'

"Well, boys, time to rethink. It is not the size of the gift but the size of the giver's heart. I am more appreciative of attitude than amount. The rich boys give of their wealth. They hardly notice that their bank balance has a smaller bottom line. Maybe they are only able to buy a single camel this week instead of two beasts, but so what. Next month, they'll add another camel to the herd. In fact, sometimes these very same church leaders cheat the widow of some of her belongings or her home, and then come marching into the temple. They whip around in their fancy robes, attract attention of the audience, and then feel so noble for their own generosity. 'My, my! Won't my neighbors and fellow business associates think I am

God fearing? I am so worthy,' as they swish, swish up to the front of the room.

"Well, my loyal dozen, those boys gave of their wealth with the wrong motive and attitude. The widow lady gave of her poverty. She gave all she had to live on that week. She may go hungry or not have funds to buy sandals for her son. Who do you think really gave a true gift of love for God and not just a gift for show? Remember, fellows, the amount is not nearly as important as the heart."

(Yes, I know the old story of the kid who came to Bible school with a quarter and a dime tightly clutched in his fist. During offering, he dropped in the dime. When asked why the dime and not the quarter, he replied, "Well, the Lord says He loves a cheerful giver. I can give the dime much more cheerfully than the quarter.")

Our widow represents a mature follower. She recognized that she was to share generously, sometimes even sacrificially. Her love for the Lord was mighty, and the Lord used her as an example.

Now let's extend the application a bit to today and our Christian response. Many of us old folks refer to ourselves as seniors, the gray-haired and wrinkled ones. We begin to think we are as useless as the widow's mite for the growth of the church. As we mature, our crooked fingers and creaking knees are unable to hike miles with the teens or tote heavy loads to help a friend move. We hesitate to volunteer to prepare food for the church potluck or to do deep cleaning of the church building. We decline to join the mission team as they travel to Afghanistan or New York to help advance the Kingdom because of lack of physical energy (or dollars). Our giving sometimes is reduced as retirement funds begin to dwindle and worries fill our balding little heads.

Mature adults may begin to doubt their usefulness for the Lord. Do we slip into services with our wobbly legs moving at the speed of a two-legged turtle and realize few folks even acknowledge our presence? We cannot sign up for nursery duty, to work at VBS, or to sing for the worship team. Many are just not physically able to do those tasks now. Woe is me. Just take me, Lord, and let the tulips grow on my grave.

Well, it is time for a mental makeover. My mature friends, your mite is worthy of worship and will be blessed of God. It is the motive and attitude of your service and gifts that count. Remember, you are not old. You are just experienced. Use that experience for the Kingdom, but perhaps in a more limited way. Find a teen and take her to lunch for conversation about spiritual opportunities and challenges. Provide a hurting member with a pair of listening ears. Remember, John was still writing while in prison at a very old age. Get out your computer and type messages of encouragement to the ministry staff or church volunteers. If able, prepare a simple meal for a young couple stretched to the breaking point as they struggle to work and provide for a young family.

"Poor me" is not an acceptable Christian attitude. Out of your rocking chair and onto your work stool. You are still vital to growth of the Kingdom. You just need to open up the eyes and find new ways of service. These are our encore years. Make them the most profitable time of your life. You don't have to go to work at eight o'clock in the morning. You have 365 days of vacation. Are you going to waste them? Not if the Lord continues to give you breath. He has a plan for you. You are tough and experienced. Don't let anyone minimize your potential. Just readjust and redirect. Use your talents and experience, but in a new manner. You may have only a penny's worth of energy left, but don't waste it.

**Pray for God's guidance as you reenlist for service.
There is might with our mite as we
mature. Recognize it. Go for it.**

Are You Ill? Hydrocephalus?
Maybe Spiritual Anemia?

WHAT IS THE STATE of your health? Do you worry about cancer, arthritis, or ingrown toenails? Are medical bills hanging over you like the sword of Damocles? Has senioritis confined you to the rocker or brought on the blues? Physical health issues have confronted folks forever. Peter's fever-plagued mother-in-law needed help. Naaman had a bout of leprosy. A disease took the life of Lazarus. Physical sickness is dreadful. Youth is frustrated with immobility or hospital stays. College students get behind in studies when ill. Workers miss necessary income when confined with flu. Jesus cared about that and certainly demonstrated His power over illness, disease, and death (Matthew 4:23).

We pray for the sick. We deliver daisies, serve soup, or send cards to friends who are ill. No one seeks illness of any type. But physical sickness is only one type of malady. What about spiritual disability? In Matthew 9:10–13, when asked why His disciples ate with tax collectors and sinners, Jesus replied, "It is not the healthy who need a doctor, but the sick. But go and learn what this means: 'I desire mercy, not sacrifice.' For I have not come to call the righteous, but sinners." Apparently, Jesus is concerned about our spiritual health.

I found an interesting article written by Stanley Paregien for the *Christian Standard* (March 15, 1969). Paregien listed a number of spiritual ills that inflict many of us. I have attempted to define them in a rather personal manner. Perhaps you will join me in a spiritual checkup. Diagnose your own soul. Do you have one or more of the following problems? Be honest with yourself. Don't worry about your spouse, friend, or neighbor.

This is a self-check challenge. Perhaps you will even redefine some of the ailments based on your personal experiences.

1. **Spiritual Anemia:** Your zip and zeal for engagement with the Word has disappeared. Bible study class is missing from your calendar. Enthusiastic volunteering on Kingdom projects around the community has vanished. You look pale and haggard Sundays at church, but recreational or work responsibilities on Monday find you eager and alive. Maybe you've even resorted to a slumberland service at home. What is your status?

2. **Spiritual Rigor Mortis:** This is a highly communicable virus that makes petrified statues out of once-productive saints. With this disease, immobility, inactivity, and the word *no* fill their lives. No committee work. No helping tutor students. No baking pies for church funerals. These folks are really ready for the rocking chair and funeral planning. Spiritual death is near. Which word is found more frequently in your vocabulary, yes or no?

3. **Spiritual Xerophthalmia (Dry Eyes):** This disorder makes you emotionally sterile. No tears for you over hurting folks, overworked church staff, home-alone children, unchurched youth, or physically ailing church family. Just dry eyes and hard hearts. Remember, "as [Christ] approached Jerusalem and saw the city, [He] wept over it" (Luke 19:41).

4. **Spiritual Hydrocephalus (Cranial Enlargement):** This creeps up on its victims as they experience some success in their lives, causing them to get a big head. Results include delusions of grandeur (Romans 12:16–17). Folks with this disease only want to be involved with tasks that allow the spotlight to shine upon their faces. Washing dishes, trimming hedges, or sewing crib blankets are for less-able folks. Out front and public is the name of their game. Does your head require a hat several sizes larger than normal? Hmm! Maybe you need to take a moment and experience some behind-the-scene tasks that need completing. Go for it.

5. **Spiritual Hyperacusis (Sound Sensitivity):** Folks afflicted with this disease are hypersensitive to criticism of their own faults or even the hard truth about controversial spiritual topics. A common reaction (stated or implied) to tough-love comments is, "Don't tell me that," or "I know best," or perhaps, "You have the scripture all

wrong." Paul reminded Timothy, "For the time will come when men will not put up with sound doctrine. Instead, to suit their own desires, they will gather around them a great number of teachers to say what their itching ears want to hear" (2 Timothy 4:3–4). Are you quick to criticize others but cringe when the tables are turned?

6. **Spiritual Tetanus (Lockjaw):** There are two forms of this disease: constant "open mouth and insert foot" and "continual locked, closed mouth." Examples include failing to ever spread the Word, witness, or show verbal love for others. Timidity or verbalized excuses sneak out of our mouth, such as "I don't know enough. Let someone else speak out." Do you ever experience Christian lockjaw?

The time has come for you to visit the Perfect Physician: Jesus. Pray for healing. Seek help from other Christians. Renew your faith. Avoid spiritual starvation. Have a desire to be healed. Associate with healthy Christ followers. Review your list of friends and decide if they are helping or hurting your spiritual health.

Live long for the Lord.

"I Want to Be Just Like You"

DOLLY IN *FAMILY CIRCUS* (January 23, 2017) expressed my thoughts rather well: "Mommy, if I ever get a sister, I want her to be just like you." My prayer would be, "Mother, when I grow up, I want to be just like you." Yes, of course, one must desire to be like Christ (Philippians 2:1–11), but for an earthly model, my mother was ideal.

Simple, quiet, kind, and God-fearing describes Mom. Unlike her daughter, she never said (and I assume never thought) an unkind word. Even though Dad was extremely quiet, he was tough around the edges, and he often responded with ungentle remarks.

My father was an engineer who worked in the field for the US Geological Survey (mapping department of our government). His work necessitated moving with great frequency. As a young child in the 1930s, those moves happened about every four to six weeks. My model, my mother, would pack all our belongings into the family car and the government pickup, and off we went. While Father worked, she had to find housing, stores, doctors, and church for the family of four. Never did I hear her complain. As I matured, I realized what a difficult, challenging life she experienced.

Later, as we advanced in school, we moved to Rolla, Missouri, and Mother became a quiet, behind-the-scenes pillar in Ridgeview Christian Church. Her love extended not only to our family but to the entire church family. Rich memories fill me with both joy and tears as I reflect on her short time on this earth. Perhaps God needed her more than I did. Someday I would love to chat with God about that decision of His. I think I needed her influence for more than just a quarter of a century.

For many, thinking about Mother's Day brings joy and celebration. For others, tears, sadness, or even anger fills their thoughts. Jesus, as He hung on the cross, obviously was very thoughtful of His mother. He looked down at John and assigned him the responsibility of caring for a newly adopted mom (John 19:25–27). What love that exhibits. His actions, however, suddenly provide Mary with a new responsibility becoming a maternal role model for John and the other disciples.

As we search the scriptures for mothers to remember, several pop into our memory. Hannah, after years of waiting, gave birth to Samuel. While praying to God for a child, she promised that if motherhood were to happen, she would dedicate the child to God. Keeping her promise, she brought Samuel at a very young age to the temple, presenting him to Eli, the priest, with these words: "As surely as you live, my lord, I am the woman who stood here beside you praying to the Lord. I prayed for this child, and the Lord has granted me what I asked of him. So now I give him to the Lord. For his whole life he will be given over to the Lord" (1 Samuel 1:26–28). I cannot imagine what love and tears were required of Hannah as she left her son behind. However, that love example filled Samuel's heart in later years, helping him become a wonderful leader. Perhaps Samuel said, "I just wanted to be like you, Mom."

Not all mother memories are beautiful. Mothers are imperfect, just like nonmothers, for we have all sinned. Mother Rebekah gave birth to twin boys. Papa Isaac loved Esau, but Mama Rebekah preferred Jacob. When time came for distribution of the family birthright, conniving Mama cheated the elder twin Esau out of his birthright as the senior child. Although it was undoubtedly God's will that Jacob the younger be given the leadership position, Rebekah would not have been my choice for mother-of-the-year award (Genesis 25:20–34).

Eve lost one of her sons because of the hatred and jealousy Cain had for brother Abel. As you remember, Cain killed his sibling one day in the field just because Abel brought more preferable offerings to God and was looked on with favor by Him as a result. That mother must have shed many tears during the solitude of the night (Genesis 4:2–16). The life of moms can be most difficult when children fail to exhibit appropriate behaviors.

One might also wonder if Eve ever pondered, "What did I do wrong that my son Cain failed to model my love for his sibling?"

As you honor your mother, either personally or in your memory, remember that today is one of empty memories for some. Parent separation, divorce, premature death, or abandonment leave a void of hugs, kisses, kindnesses, or caring. Foster children often are shuffled around with only a bag of harsh, unloving, and sometimes cruel mother thoughts. Perhaps you even know of a friend who was homeless and slept in the family car. Those scenarios often create nightmares, not warm, fuzzy, heartfelt love.

Are you among the blessed with a wonderful mom? If yes, give thanks to the Lord. But also—a final challenge—find someone in your life (your natural child or adopt a lonely one) you can love and be a model to. Pray that you may then hear them say,

"I want to be just like you."

Abba Father, the Most High God (El Elyon)

Creator, El Shaddai, Everlasting Father

ANNUALLY, WE CELEBRATE FATHER'S Day. Many names for our heavenly father come to mind. The scriptures are full of descriptive terms for God:

- Father of Compassion (2 Corinthians 1:3)
- God of Glory (Acts 7:2)
- Father of Our Lord Jesus Christ (Colossians 1:3)
- God of Israel (Matthew 15:31)
- Father of Lights (James 1:17)
- God of Peace (Hebrews 13:20)

God of All Comfort, the All-Sufficient God, King of Kings.

Thank You, Father, for Your love, watchful eye, and caring concern. Today, we celebrate all fathers.

Church history also remembers many dads with a variety of super characteristics

1. **Prodigal Son's Papa:** He welcomed his wayward son home after the kid acknowledged his selfish ways. The door was flung open and a party evolved, even though it irritated big brother. Love is not

withheld by God when His children return home. So also should earthly fathers continue to reach out to wandering offspring, whether they left for a time of pleasure or selfishness. But just as this father reconnected with the prodigal, he also communicated with the elder son who stayed home to run the farm. Open lines of communication at home are essential for a God-fearing family.

2. **Sampson:** He made tragic choices but eventually triumphed as he utilized his superman strength to help his family. Romans 3:23 reminds us that all "fall short of the glory of God." Men of God ask forgiveness and move forward, knowing God wants to walk by their side. Be a man. Take God's hand. Then lead boldly as a role model.

3. **Jarius:** He was a dad with extreme faith and stick-to-itiveness, who aggressively followed Jesus in order to provide for his daughter. He encountered crowds, delays, and probably taunts from others as he attempted to get close to Jesus. Caring fathers extend their energies as they provide for the family, despite a pile of challenges. Keep focused. Continue to follow the Master. Don't be sidetracked by taunts and challenges from Satan's pals. You are the dad. Let the family count on you.

4. **Joseph:** Jesus's stepfather followed God's directions for his life with humility and positive action. Certainly, Joseph experienced disapproval from his Jewish friends prior to the birth of Jesus. Often being a God-fearing papa is a tough job. Don't give up. Celebrate your life as a Christian. Hang tough. Do all things with love and kindness, minus anger.

5. **Job:** While experiencing excruciating pain, he still called out, "I know that my Redeemer lives, and that in the end he will stand upon the earth" (Job 19:25–27). Do not become discouraged in times of mental or physical pain. Your faith must remain strong both for your own salvation and as a rigorous model for your family. God supported Job. Dad, He is still there for you.

Dad, where do you connect with these leaders? Where does your father line up with this parade of positive male parents?

Is your dad like the Prodigal Son's Papa, Sampson, Jarius, Joseph, or Job? Hopefully, your father is a combination of the best behaviors of each.

Thank you, dads, for all you do for your family.

Bucket List Completed

Wednesday, June 29, 2016:
Longtime Dream Fulfilled

SINCE GRADUATION FROM COLLEGE, my bucket list had contained two items: milk a cow and fly a plane. During the year of the Bicentennial, Sandburg School had a milk cow on their site. I sat on a little stool and did three swishes of milk into the bucket. Item number one accomplished. But what about two—fly a plane?

The years passed, and it just seemed like an impossible opportunity. Then, out of the blue, friends made an offer I absolutely could not refuse.

In exchange for a hot dog roast and pontoon ride, they would take me up in a plane and turn the controls over to me for a short trip. The evening was perfect. No wind. Gorgeous clouds. The view was spectacular. As we returned home from the Bloomington-Normal Airport later, the lights in Decatur and Springfield cheered us onward.

Although my heart thumped a couple of extra beats as the controls were switched over to the novice copilot, it was an exhilarating experience. Patience paid off, and fifty-eight years after college, we were cruising through the blue sky. How joyful can one be?

At least one other item, however, remains on my bucket—an event with far more lasting joy. As Paul said in Philippians 1:21–24 (RSV), "For to me to live is Christ, and to die is gain. If it is to be life in the flesh, that means fruitful labor for me. Yet which I shall choose I cannot tell. I am hard pressed between the two. My desire is to depart and be with Christ, for that is far better. But to remain in the flesh is more necessary on your account." Paul's wish list was mixed. He so desired to enjoy His reward in heaven, but serving others was vital for Kingdom expansion.

Serving Christ by caring for His flock here on earth is a wonderful and rewarding opportunity. Daily, Paul was sharing the gospel. "To live is Christ" means imitating the example of Christ and advertising that message to your contacts in the coffee shop, the law offices, and the ballpark. Paul adds that living Christ means pursuing the knowledge of Christ. Not just a set of facts about Christ, but to know Christ as a person. "I want to know Christ and the power of his resurrection and the fellowship of sharing in his sufferings, becoming like him in his death, and so, somehow, to attain to the resurrection from the dead" (Philippians 3:10–11). My bucket list just has to include serving Him and simultaneously, eagerly anticipating wearing the white robe while singing, "Holy, Holy," and smiling at the Lord.

How vigorously do you live Christ daily while also earnestly pursuing an eternity in the holy city, with God sitting on His throne? This glorious city is not for the cowardly and faithless idolaters, liars, and other folks who have turned their backs on Christ. Check your life and actions today. Are you in sync with Him? Then take out your own bucket list and add one more item: joining Christ in the New Jerusalem. I have it on my list. I can hardly wait. I hope it does not take another fifty-eight years.

Today, I walk with God. Someday, I will fly away with Him.
Come along and join me.

The Bible: One Bald Man, Two Ferocious Bears, Forty-Two Young Men

What a title. Children's fairy tale? Incident at a
local zoo? College frat party? Fake news?
Nope! Straight from God's Word.

AN INTERESTING PIECE FROM the May 23, 2017, *Balli Report*, a church
humor newsletter, passed by my eyes. Why would we think about baldness
and bears in relation to the Bible? Well, in 2 Kings 2:22–23, Elisha the
prophet became the object of ridicule from a group of young men. Elisha,
relatively young but apparently follically challenged, was a prophet of God.
Elijah, his mentor, was suddenly taken to heaven in a whirlwind. Elisha

loved him like a father but saw him no more. He was now on his own. What will happen?

Picking up the cloak of Elijah, which fell to the ground as he disappeared into heaven, Elisha becomes the new messenger of God. Immediately he meets a challenge. The men of the city of Jericho tell him their water is contaminated. The power of God allows Elisha to miraculously cleanse it. His credentials established, Elisha takes a hike to Bethel.

Suddenly, as his sandals crunch the rocky path, some youth (probably teenagers) start heckling him. Perhaps they heard of his message and miracle in Jericho. Perhaps they were just bored. Whatever. Satan was working through them.

They yelled out, "Go on up, you bald head!" And then they repeated the jeer, "Go on up, you bald head!"

Wow, that would tick me off. We don't know if he had a religious vow requiring him to shave his head or if he was just prematurely bald. Apparently, however, the top of his head was hairless.

Now what would you have done, dear reader? You have just donned the cloak of the famous prophet Elijah. Your first act in spreading the message of God was to perform a miracle. You do not have a diploma from Jericho College of the Bible. Your training is limited to an internship with the mighty messenger Elijah. I imagine I would be shaking in my sandals, wondering what in the world am I to do now. What message does God want me to share to bring His people closer to Him?

The echo of the forty-two loud-mouthed teens runs through his head: "Bald head! Bald head!" He turns and gives them the old teacher stare and then calls a curse on them in the name of the Lord. This would not be a string of swear words, but more of a promise of trouble. Yes, trouble.

Guess who is there to help him? The Lord kicks into action a pair of bears, who dash out of the woods and attack the mob of teens. Elisha continues his journey. God is praised, and I suppose the boys go home to find boxes of Band-Aids and to lick their wounds. Perhaps in the future, each will show greater respect to God's servants.

So what is the message from this bloody story? When we reject God's message or show disrespect to His messengers, we need to rethink our actions. Are we scorning, challenging, denying, or ignoring the Word of God? No, I don't think bears will leap out of the bushes and nibble on our ears if we are. But if we have friends who reject His Word, warn them that

God means business when He says, "Love me." Maybe you wink at some of God's commands or become complacent in loving your irritating neighbor or caring for the ill. Not good.

Second, be assured that as a messenger for God, He will give you courage and ultimately protect you as you teach or visit with a friend or colleague in need of comfort, guidance, counseling, or just knowledge about the saving grace of Christ.

Don't let Satan take over your mind. Let the bears of God guard you as you bravely step out of your comfort zone and tell others about God's love.

Be bold. Be brave.

Memories and Memorial

THE SHOES ON THE Danube Promenade is a memorial in Budapest, Hungary, on the shores of the Danube. The sculptor, Gyula Pauer, created it to honor the Budapest Jews who were killed by fascist Arrow Cross militiamen in Budapest during World War II. Approximately thirty-five hundred people were ordered to take off their shoes and were shot at the edge of the water so that their bodies fell into the river and were washed away. Sixty pairs of period-appropriate shoes made of iron represent the people killed on January 8, 1945. A sign reminds all: "To the memory of the victims shot into the Danube by Arrow Cross Militiamen in 1944–45. Erected April 16, 2005." For further information and photos google, shoes on the Danube Promenade and you will find several sites.

Christians also remember. We remember the ghastly death and sacrifice of the Lord. His death was as horrific as that of the Jews in

Budapest. He suffered an atrocious death on a cross with nails in His hands and feet and a sword thrust into His side. Weekly, we honor His memory when we eat of the bread and drink of the wine, a symbol of His broken body and shed blood.

Silence accompanies visitors' arrival at the memorial on the water's edge. Candles often twinkle, evoking memories of lost loved ones. Prayers are uttered. Adults whisper bits of history into the ears of the young, passing on the torch of remembrance to another generation. Perhaps a visitor will spot a tear in the eye of a senior leaning on a cane, recalling the special occasion of a long-lost loved one. The brain tumbles with a variety of thoughts: anger, sadness, tenderness, or maybe loneliness. This is a sacred time of respect for those who have gone before.

Let's stop and think about the behavior and actions of Christians today as we reflect during communion. Do our minds zip back to that time when Christ was hung on display for gamblers, gawkers, and tearful family members and followers to view? Can we shed a tiny tear as we reflect on His mother weeping on the sidelines? Would we have been willing to place the body in a tomb designed for ourselves? Would you have had the courage to go to the burial site to pay respects and then dash to tell others of the empty tomb?

More importantly, what do you do during communion time each Lord's Day? Do you remember that He sacrificed His life willingly? He was not forced to this death. Are prayers on your lips and maybe even a tear in your eye as you silently focus on the bread and wine symbols? In 1 Corinthians 11:17–34, Paul encourages the Corinthian church members to remember the night of the betrayal of the Lord. Jesus had taken the bread and told the guys at the table, "This is my body, which is for you; do this in remembrance of me." Then He took the cup and commented, "This cup is the new covenant in my blood; do this, whenever you drink it, in remembrance of me" (1 Corinthians 11:24). Paul's memo from Ephesus to the church in Corinth is straightforward: Remember His death and resurrection. Not only is it an appropriate way to draw you closer to the Lord, but it is a wonderful witness to those around you when you respectfully remember.

Paul has one last warning: eating and drinking of this bread and cup in an unworthy manner (failing to remember the death, burial, and resurrection) is bringing judgement upon yourself.

Therefore, friends, time for introspection. What do you do during communion? Pray? Request forgiveness for sins during the week? Hum along with the music playing? Think about lunch plans or take a quick mental nap? Shed a tear? Check your cell phone?

Do not partake haphazardly, but soberly. May those shoes on the river's edge cause you to reflect and review your behavior during the Lord's Supper.

This is a moment for remembrance.

Return of the White Pelicans

RECENTLY, I GLANCED OUT our kitchen window and squealed silently with delight at a glorious sight: the return of the white pelicans. Like a ballet company, approximately one hundred of these gorgeous creatures were calmly swimming, dipping bills in unison into the water, and gulping down fish from Lake Springfield. They forage for small fish in shallow water; our spot on the lake was perfect, as the drought had resulted in shallow water. On the average, each bird eats about four pounds of food a day. Fishermen, however, are probably distressed, as these feathered friends provide competition for their own catch.

Weighing between nine and thirty pounds with an average wingspan of ninety-five inches, making graceful, flapping sounds, these orange-billed birds glide, dip, and flutter their wings. Perhaps we might consider a comparison between these rare fowl and Christians.

Young pelicans are hunted by great horned owls and bald eagles. Lake Springfield has bald eagles, so I'm confident that the senior members of the pelican family keep a watchful eye on the young. We, too, as members of the Body of Christ must be diligent in our watching out for newborn Christians of whatever age. We know Satan moves around as a "roaring lion, looking for someone to devour" (1 Peter 5:8). Are we circling the wagons and lending a hand to a youthful child of God? When doubts arise, are we each prepared to encourage and support their questions and wonderings? As children of God stumble, we need to lend a hand of encouragement. Don't close your eyes and say, "Oh, well. She is just a kid. Let her have her time of revelry. I have better things to do than looking after a stumbling Christian. Besides, I have many Christian friends, so why connect with a newbie?"

Shame on us if we fail to help. Unanswered questions, missteps, and changed behaviors to be Christlike do not come easily to the newborn. In fact, even we who have been Christ followers for years stumble. Become a big brother or sister to a new child of God, regardless of your age or theirs. Reach out and begin to build relationships with a youth of today. Encourage. Model. Mentor. Love.

In 1981, the white pelican was placed on the endangered species list. Ornithologists became concerned because breeding areas were disappearing. Excessive spraying of DDT and other factors also contributed to their worries. The good news is that pelican population is recovering.

A recent article in *The Ambassador* (Ozark Christian College) by President Matthew Proctor reported some shocking statistics. Americans who claim "no religious affiliation" have increased among our youthful citizens. In a recent survey, 11 percent of Builders (born 1928–1945) claimed no connection with any religious group versus 53 percent of Generation Zs (born after 1997). Less than half of Generation Zs find the need for a relationship with God. Are Christians becoming an endangered species?

Are we as concerned about diminishing numbers of followers of Christ as bird lovers are of vanishing pelicans? What about your grandchild, young relative, or angry neighbor kid? Do we care enough to help change the environment that will reach out to these twenty-year-olds? Who have you adopted to mentor and disciple? Remember, Jesus is the one who can provide real love and hope.

As a final bird connection, a friend reminded me of the Master's teaching in Matthew 6:25–34, "Therefore I tell you, do not worry about your life, what you will eat or drink.... Look at the birds of the air; they do not sow or reap or store away in barns, yet your heavenly Father feeds them.... Are you not much more valuable than they?"

Of course, we are. And that includes you.
Reach out.

What Have You Swallowed Lately?
A True Story

A RECENT TRIP TO the dentist found me almost upside down in the chair while an implant was being prepared for implanting. Suddenly, I felt a very real urge to either swallow or die choking. I chose the former and preceded to swallow. After two attempts, the item blocking my breathing seemed to disappear. I looked up at the dentist and inquired, "What did I just swallow?"

His face had the strangest look as he replied, "You just swallowed my screwdriver." Now what does one do? At first, I did not believe him, but then I asked, "How big was it?" Apparently, it was rather small. To this day, I have yet to learn its exact size. When going through the airport one day, the TSA screener asked if I had any metal parts and should not pass through the x-ray machine. I replied, "Well, that is funny you should ask. I do not have any artificial joints, but I did swallow a metal screwdriver recently. Do you suppose your machine could check for that?" The wonderful lady replied, "Let's see." She told me to walk through. Reaching the other side, she smiled and said nothing was evident. I hope that is true.

So what have you swallowed? The Lord had an interesting comment as he chewed out the scribes and Pharisees one day. They pretended to be so righteous by dressing in robes and telling folks what to do, but failing to follow their own rules or in general just being hypocrites. This little sermon is recorded in Matthew 23. A sample of that tongue-lashing includes, "Woe to you, scribes and Pharisees, hypocrites! for you tithe mint and dill and cumin, and have neglected the weightier matters of the law, justice and mercy and faith; these you ought to have done, without neglecting the others." And then this famous line: "You blind guides, straining out a gnat and swallowing a camel" (Matthew 23:23–24 RSV).

Thankfully, I only swallowed a screwdriver. But what did the Lord intend for us to learn from His message to the religious leaders? Are we guilty of swallowing the camel but avoiding the small insect? Are we more concerned about frivolous details around the church rather than lost folk? Are bumpy, lumpy parking lots or the size of the coffee cups higher on our grumble list than youth in our congregation who need support, mentors, or even a scholarship to camp? Do we worry more about the volume of the guitars than the message of the lyrics?

Where do we each place our time and energy? Are we willing to call on the sick and lonely, or do we prefer eating pizza with friends? Pizza is a favorite, but if I want to avoid swallowing Christian camels, I must include the needs of hurting people as well as feeding my face.

Jesus reminded us that we too often neglect important matters that deal with justice, mercy, and faithfulness. He continued his sermon, saying, "If anyone would come after me, he must deny himself and take up his cross and follow me" (Matthew 16:24). Jesus wants zealous followers but not the selective zealousness of the Pharisees. They had folks count out nine mint leaves and then give the tenth to the Lord. We sometimes shout out for prayer in the schools, but then, how many of us have prayed with a friend or grandchild during the week and not just on Sunday? We tackle the big issue over which we have little control but fail to model and practice the very thing we are wanting schools to do: pray daily with youth. Hmmm.

It is easy to stand for or against big issues or sign a petition. It takes real commitment, however, to live out in real life what we publicly shouted for. Telling others to implement some moral message is commendable, but more important is our personal implementation of that message.

So, my friends, I hope never to swallow another dental implement. I also pray that each of us will review our own actions and make certain we are swallowing (doing) the important things that the Lord requires, not just the easy tasks.

The Glorious Eighties: What Is the Reality of Eightieth?

I CAN HEAR SOMEONE think in a discouraging way, *By the time you turn eighty, there aren't many New Year celebrations ahead for you. Call the caterer and plan a giant party for family and friends on January 1.*

My heart sank with disappointment. Was the end that close, especially as my birthday cake had eighty-three candles burning away? Should I roll up my tent, buy a new rocker and wooly slippers, and pen some goodbye, I love you cards? Being the stubborn gray hair that I am, I decided further investigation was appropriate.

As I pondered the downside of eight decades of living, an interview on *The Today Show* caught me off guard. I found myself watching Jane Fonda, and guess what information was shared? She was eighty years old. I turned to a friend and said, "Wish I were that beautiful at eighty-plus. No apparent wrinkles, gray hair, or aching muscles in her slender frame. What happened to me?" Certainly, eighty does not mean the end of life. Our eight-decade Ms. Fonda was discussing her recently released film with Robert Redford. Now that is a bit of encouragement. There must be life after eighty.

The Bible has many references to eighty. John speaks about the great hailstones weighing nearly eighty pounds each, which fell from the sky on the people. That didn't sound very pleasant. In fact, the verse continues, "They cursed God on account of the plague of hail, because the plague was so terrible" (Revelation 16:21).

Continuing my search, I discovered that Daniel was eighty at the time of a banquet given by Belshazzar. In fact, Daniel was so alert at party time that, with God's help, he interpreted the prophecy written on the wall of the royal palace (Daniel 5:25–28). Now this sounds much more exciting. Who wouldn't enjoy being invited to a royal banquet and nibbling a royal drumstick or sweet grapes with the leader of the land? Apparently also at eighty, some are still able to use their brain and interpret puzzles. Daniel provides much more encouragement to the senior.

Moses, the leader of the Israelites, was eighty and Aaron eighty-three when they stood before Pharaoh and his officials, demanding that the Children of Israel be released from slavery to go into the wilderness to pray (Exodus 7:1–7). Even though God had to speak rather firmly to the brothers, they acted with confidence in a very tough situation. Evidently, gray-headed folks are still able to take leadership roles, be responsible, and work actively for the Kingdom. Of course, if you want to just rest in the sun and play tiddlywinks, Moses is not your role model. Imagine leading a group estimated from six hundred thousand to two million-plus persons on foot over rocky, sandy, mountainous land and providing for their needs (with God's help, of course). Moses had to be a tough eighty-year-old.

Seems to me that being eighty is far preferred to forty. Reviewing the numbers, the scriptures are filled with more discouraging news for the number forty. God had Noah experience forty days and forty nights floating around in a large boat with smelly animals. Jesus was tempted in the desert for forty days. Moses spent forty years on the desert sands after killing the Egyptian, and the Israelites wandered forty years in the wilderness. I'm delighted that forty is history in my life.

More good news, however, about eighty: The Children of Israel, after being tested in the wilderness and fighting off many enemy tribes, experienced peace for eighty years (Judges 3:30). "Blessed are the peacemakers, for they will be sons of God" (Matthew 5:9). Proverbs 16:31 tells us, "Gray hair is a crown of splendor; it is attained by a righteous life." Paul in 2 Corinthians 4:16 says, "Therefore we do not lose heart. Though outwardly we are wasting away, yet inwardly we are being renewed day by day." Finally, David pens these words of encouragement: "The length of our days is seventy years—or eighty; if we have the strength" (Psalm 90:10).

Enjoy your mature years. Serve faithfully. Be prepared to fly away to be with Him.

The Prayer Bubble

Nine Possible Areas to Raise up Prayer for Sunday Ministry

A FRIEND FORWARDED A piece by Kim Butts of Harvest Prayer Ministries. Although written in 2014, I believe the ideas are still relevant for today. Sundays can be rough as families prepare for church. Workers are often tense as they anticipate their part in the service. New folks arrive, wary that no one will greet them. Worshippers enter with "heavy baggage of worry, depression, anger or fatigue." The author suggests we develop a Prayer Bubble over the service for Holy Spirit protection. Begin prayer for each soul.

This writer has edited the ideas, but they are based on the original piece. Perhaps each of you will take a moment and find at least two ideas with which you can assist. Get your Prayer Bubble launched. Thought should be given to developing teams to help implement these suggestions in your church.

1. **Prepare Prior to Sunday:** Organize prayer teams designed to pray for each person by name in your congregation, including staff. This will be tough for a large church, but develop teams assigned to several families and individuals. Encourage teams to pray specifically, by name, for all on the list that they will be

blessed by the service and touched to go forward and live the life of a Christ follower the next seven days. Repeat weekly.

2. **Develop First Arrival Intercession:** Engage parking lot attendants and greeters in the Prayer Bubble program. These folks not only assist people arriving but also smile and make folks feel welcome. Friendly handshakes and greetings as folks arrive set the stage for the rest of the service. Now, add one additional responsibility for these Welcome Warriors. Teach them to pray silently for people as they enter. Pray for peace, joy in worship, restoration of the soul, forgiveness for weekly errors, and especially that each will have a wonderful refreshing of spirit and soul through worship and fellowship.

3. **Provide Prayer Team Volunteers:** Volunteers can be identified by wearing a badge or tag identifying themselves as people who may be approached if there is a prayer need. These folks will immediately move to a quiet area and pray with anyone who wishes to connect to a prayer warrior. Prayers will generally be short, but follow-up may be arranged if appropriate. The key, however, is to remain visible and available to anyone needing to share a burden.

4. **Involve the Building and Grounds Staff:** Surprised to see this? Who better to learn how to prepare the building for spiritual cleansing for worshippers than the cleaning staff? As they scrub, dust, mow, and sweep, request that they pray while moving around the building and grounds. Staff may request God's presence and blessing to surround the property where formal and informal worship takes place. Draft these dedicated workers for God's prayer team.

5. **Engage the Communion Prep Squad and Servers:** As communion is prepared, let the workers send up petitions for each person remembering Christ's sacrifice. When servers distribute the trays, encourage each to pray for those in the pews to feel God's presence. Silent petitions for a lonely stranger, discouraged mother, or distraught youth will help the individuals take the bread and the cup in a worthy manner as peace settles over them.

6. **Don't Forget the Ushers:** People who hand out bulletins, show people to their seats, or just say, "Howdy," to a stranger or longtime member may silently pray for each person. Pray that God's love will cover them as they participate in the service.

7. **Create a Special Team to Pray for Behind-the-Scene Operations:** This team moves around the building, praying that the sound system and other technology will operate smoothly. Prayer for smooth operation of all components of the service will allow increased honor and glory to God, as folks can focus on the message, not the mechanics. Simple task. Short prayers. This is a super opportunity for new prayer warriors, including our teens or new members.

8. **Provide for Pre-Service Intercession:** Select a team to find a quiet location prior to the service and pray for teachers, youth, the ministering staff, and each person attending worship that Sunday. Pray that the power of the Holy Spirit will move people, causing them to assess their own life. Pray that the service will be pleasing to the Lord. Pray for visitors and regular attenders alike. Pray for joy, celebration, forgiveness, and spiritual awakening.

9. **Consider a Prayer Team during the Service:** Perhaps each week, a team of two may pray silently for the actual worship service as it unfolds. Pray for the team on stage as well as for members of the audience, that each will be filled with the spirit. Pray that grace and forgiveness may be part of the hearts of each. Pray for changed lives and hearts.

Start this coming Lord's Day. Be part of the Prayer Bubble.

Southpaw Assassinates Fat King

Can't Remember Where He Left His Sword

A WONDERFUL, GORY STORY especially delightful for twelve-year-old guys, a story even more exciting than modern-day tales. Perhaps your memory needs refreshing. The Israelites were complaining again to the Lord for deliverance from their enemies. Get us out from under the thumb of King Eglon, they petitioned. We find in Judges 3:12–30 how God intervened and rescued them from oppression.

God sent them a left-handed deliverer, a young buck by the name of Ehud. Ehud's skills included swordsmanship. Before leaving home, he crafted his own weapon—a two-edged sword about eighteen inches long. Strapping the wicked weapon to his right hip, he covered it up with his shirt. Taking off to Moab, he arrived at the palace and, following proper etiquette, presented a tribute (gift) to the king. If the guards had checked the guy out for weapons, they would probably have missed the sword, as they'd have been looking for it on his left side. Remember: You reach across your body to grab the sword. He is left-handed, so it is on his right. Also, there were no metal detectors in those days.

Then the action begins. Our daring swordsman empties the tent of all servants, saying he needs to whisper a secret to His Majesty. He tells the king he has a message from God and sidles up to him in his summer palace. As the king stands up to greet Ehud, Ehud reaches under his tunic, and out comes the sword. Immediately, he plunges it into the king's fat tummy. King Eglon needed Weight Watchers services very badly, as he was quite plump. The sword remains as Ehud pulls his hand out.

Our Israelite hero closes and locks the door and then departs for home through the back porch. The king's servants are reluctant to enter the locked room, since one never knows what a king might be doing. After some amount of time, however, they find a key and unlock the chamber, and there is their dead king. The culprit has disappeared.

Slipping home to Ephraim, Ehud rallies the hometown troops with these words: "Follow me, for the Lord has given Moab, your enemy, into your hands."

Our daredevil leads the group back to Moab. Making a long tale short, they have a successful battle, striking down over ten thousand Moabites, not allowing even one enemy to escape.

End of story. Peace in the land for eighty years. Would that could happen in our world today. And so "Lefty Kills Hefty" (Judges 3:15–30). The Children of Israel cried out for deliverance. The Lord sent Ehud, who single-handedly killed the king and led his army to overcome the enemy.

So, what twenty-first-century lesson might we take from this OT story? Maybe you, too, have demons or enemies in your life: fear? Hidden sin? Discouragement? Loneliness? Marital concerns? Diminishing love for the Lord? We probably each have some internal or external life enemy. If yes, do we grumble like the Children of Israel, or are we ready to listen to the Lord and take action? If action is your desire, look to Hebrews 4:12–13: "For the word of God is living and active. Sharper than any double-edged sword, it penetrates even to dividing soul and spirit, joints and marrow; it judges the thoughts and attitudes of the heart. Nothing in all creation is hidden from God's sight. Everything is uncovered and laid bare before the eyes of him to whom we must give account."

God knows your needs, your sins, your complaints, and your worries, just like He knew the needs and complaints of the Israelites. They grumbled, and He sent Ehud. We complain, pray for help, cry out, or worry, and He sends His Holy Spirit to comfort and care for us. No, it is probably not quite as dramatic in our lives as with the story of our sword-swishing soldier, but He will comfort us. He will send help and intervention using Christian friends as emissaries for Him. Reading His Word enhances the opportunity for the Holy Spirit to speak to you. Get your Bible two-edged sword out.

Assassinate your fears. Erase your despair.
Conquer your heart-felt enemies. Help others.
Become a swordsman for the Lord.

Wise Guys Take a Long Road Trip—Not Just a Weekend

Wise Guys Make Wise Decisions, Take Off to Unknown. Wise Folks Today Duplicate Decisions of the Wise Men

SHEEP, DONKEY, STRAW, STARS, baby, robe-draped parents—these images flash before us continually during the Christmas season. Lumbering along with these favorites, we also view plodding camels loaded down with rich-looking scholars carrying presents. What do we know about these worshippers? Why did these wise guys make the trip and leave their jobs behind? Should they be bending knees by the Messiah's crib? Take a moment and read Matthew 2:1–12.

Biblical scholars suggest that in our eagerness to celebrate the early visitors to see the promised King, we perhaps have rushed the arrival of the astrologers. Research suggests that this group of Oriental scientists came east from Babylon or maybe Persia (Iran). The trip of several hundred miles would have been slow going over sand and mountains. No Crown Plazas in which to rest or golden arches to provide nourishment. Their GPS was a star in the sky. They probably had armed men and servants along to protect them and care for their needs. These were the first known followers from another nation (Gentiles) to worship the King.

To confirm the final destination of their travels, a personal visit to King Herod, located in Jerusalem, was required. The boss called together all the Jewish religious leaders and students of history to find the answer as to where this new king was to be born. These bright scholars responded, "In Bethlehem in Judea, … for this is what the prophet has written" (Matthew 2:5, Micah 5:2). Providing the Magi with this information, Herod also requested they tell him the exact location after they find the future monarch.

Now, my dear readers, do you think this little trip of several hundred miles, probably on camelback (not an American Airlines 747) over unpaved trails of sand with a side trip to Jerusalem for detailed directions, could have been made in four to six days? Sounds impossible. In addition, we know that Herod, a bloodthirsty tyrant, instructed his soldiers to kill all the male babies two years old or younger in Bethlehem.

Why kill two-year-olds if the wise men arrived while the shepherds were paying their visit to the Christ Child in the stable area? Herod knew it was a long journey. In addition, Matthew tells us that the wise men came to "the house" where they saw "the child" and His mother. Logic would suggest that their trip was about two years in length. Remember, they had to make arrangements for a long-distant jaunt.

Reviewing our memories of Christmas pageants, how many wise men do you see? Three pops into our heads. Why? Reread Matthew 2, and nowhere does it indicate the number or their names. So why three? Could it be that since the visitors brought gifts of gold, frankincense, and myrrh, we assume each gift had a single giver? There is no evidence included in Matthew's account as to the number of wise men—two, three, twenty, forty, or? All we know is that because of their study of the sky, they recognized something special. They had seen a new star—perhaps a different type star, not one that twinkled, but was a bold light in the sky. This star moved. "and the star that they had seen in the east went ahead of them until it stopped over the place where the child was" (Matthew 2:9). Once again, we need to readjust our memories.

Yes, sometimes tradition and memory mislead us. Nevertheless, these wise men should provide us with an incredible model of behavior. They believed what they saw. They prepared for a long trip in order to worship this King. They were filled with great expectation. They left all to make this journey. They brought treasured gifts, were overjoyed, and bowed down, as they worshiped the baby. They exhibited courage, faith, devotion, sacrifice, and obedience.

What about your relationship with the King? Are you overjoyed and eager to worship? Have you exhibited faith and willingness to sacrifice to follow Him? What treasured gifts of love and service have you shared? Are you a wise follower?

Wise men remember the past but eagerly press
forward. Rise up and follow His star.
Paul set the example: "Forgetting what is behind and
straining toward what is ahead, I press on toward the
goal to win the prize for which God has called me
heavenward in Christ Jesus" (Philippians 3:13b–14).

Belgian Hotel Rents Fish to Lonely Guests

YES. A NEW MARKETING tool found its way to the Hotel Charleroi Airport in Belgium for folks traveling solo. For four dollars per night, a fish is available for a visit to the room of the lonely one. This is probably quieter than providing a friendly puppy or cozy kitty (and much less messy). A quiet option could be a small stuffed animal. Hotel workers assure folks that they take "very good care of our fish."

My first reaction was, "How clever and unique." I remember the many evenings in a motel room alone while working as a nationwide reading consultant. Departing on a late Sunday evening or predawn Monday and often not returning to my own little bed until Friday, the four walls of a Comfort Inn or Best Western were my companions

for many nights. Fortunately, preparations for work the following day filled most evenings. Nevertheless, I agree, one could (and did) feel a tad lonely.

Several words popped into my head as I reflected on the concept of loneliness. Companionship, depression, emptiness, hopelessness, or isolation might fill a person's mind during her time on the road, away from friends and family. But on a more positive end of the spectrum, reflection, meditation, solitude, and just plain quiet are also associated with alone time. Which one of us has not wished for an hour for reflection, a nap, or reading without interruptions of whining puppy, noisy phone, or screams for attention by family or friends?

What do the scriptures say about loneliness? Jesus, the Master, needed quiet time. Often in the gospels, we see Him taking off to a quiet place following a large group service (e.g., feeding of the five thousand). Taking His inner crew of three or the entire dozen disciples, He went off to pray, think, and provide further in-depth in-service for His leadership team. Could His words possibly substitute for a tiny fish? Yes. These fishermen needed the Fisher of Men, not a colorful guppy. We can read His Word for comfort and companionship.

David, in Psalm 25:16, acknowledged that he was "lonely and afflicted." Humans need fellowship and connections. Friends are important, just as solitude also restores our souls. David continues in Psalm 142:1–7, "I cry aloud to the Lord. I lift up my voice to the Lord for mercy. I pour out my complaint before him; before him I tell my trouble. When my spirit grows faint within me, it is you who know my way.… No one is concerned for me. I have no refuge; no one cares for my life. I cry to you, Oh Lord; I say, 'You are my refuge, my portion in the land of the living.'" It is okay to cry out to the Lord. Share with Him your secret needs and hurts. Be comforted. In turn, comfort other lonely, hurting folks.

How many times have you felt, like David, alone or faint in spirit? No one seeming to care or to be concerned about you? Have you ever huddled in your home, alone, weary and teary? We all do sometimes, so instead of staring at a bowl of fish, cry out to the Lord. Acknowledge that He is present in your life. Remember, He is holding your hand and listening to your weeping, even when you are desperate. David ends his prayer while hidden in a cave: "Set me free from my prison, that I may praise your name." Bend your hearts and knees. Shout out sentences of praise. Be joyful for the flower in your yard or tweeting sparrow in the bush. Share your gratitude for blue skies with fluffy clouds or for your peanut butter-banana sandwich you chomped down. Think glass half-full rather than half-empty. Remember your salvation; Christ died for you. Yes, lonely you. Of course, He also died for me; so I, too, must celebrate that gift.

In Psalm 145:18–20, David finally turns his loneliness to praise: "The Lord is near to all who call on him, to all who call on him in truth. He fulfills the desires of those who fear him; he hears their cry and saves them. The Lord watches over all who love him."

Peter confirms the Lord's promise to be with us with his words in 1 Peter 5:7: "Cast all your anxiety on him because he cares for you." The author of Hebrews restates this promise in Hebrews 13:5: "Keep our lives free from the love of money and be content with what you have, because God has said, 'Never will I leave you: never will I forsake you'" (Hebrews 13:5).

You are not alone.
Chat with the Lord, not a fish.
Cry out to God.

Christian Fellowship: A Family

DURING A RECENT JOURNEY to southern Africa, we encountered hundreds of the largest of all land animals in the world—the elephants. These quiet-moving, herbivore tree-uprooters provided moments of pleasure as we watched them lumber along. Weighing up to 6.6 tons, they can consume from three hundred to six hundred pounds of food daily. The tusks of an elephant may weight up to two hundred pounds. The brain averages eleven pounds—larger than any other animal in the world. They love to swim but are one of the few four-legged animals that can't run.

The most wonderful part, however, is the community aspect of their lives. These mammals live in tight matriarchal herds of eight or more related females. The calves are raised and protected by the entire herd. Babies are born blind and rely upon their mothers for help. While watching a herd swim across a lake, we noted one baby struggle and dip under the water. Immediately, an older family member swam around behind and appeared to give the wee one a push forward toward the bank. The group sticks together, often showing emotion during times of stress or joy, according to elephant experts.

We, too, are members of a family. In Romans 12:5, Paul reminds us, "So we, though many, are one body in Christ, and individually members one of another." We're members of God's family; Paul continues, "So then, as we have opportunity, let us do good to everyone, and especially to those who are of the household of faith" (Galatians 6:10 RSV).

Families care, hurt, cry, encourage, support, discipline, hold hands, celebrate, gather together to show love. "If one member suffers, all suffer together; if one member is honored, all rejoice together" (1 Corinthians 12:26 RSV). Family members are never perfect. We even get grumpy with each other, but the next dawn, we jump out of bed, wash our face, and begin again. Just as the baby elephant needed a little push of encouragement while swimming, so do our Christian family and friends.

Now is the perfect time to renew connections with family members in this hour of uncertainty in our world. Introduce yourself to strangers in your church or neighborhood. Create opportunities for small gatherings of adopted aunts, cousins, or in-laws. Watch for folks needing a bit of attention or friendship, maybe even some snow removal, a lawn raked, or childcare support. Invite a new friend for coffee, a ballgame, an adult Bible fellowship class, a fishing outing, or a sewing group. Send a little note or surprise them with a homemade chocolate cake. Reach out. Initiate the action. As you hug your new friend, bonds of Christian love will form.

We are family.
Which of us will be the first to adopt a new friend?
I hope it is you.

The Starfish Story

Based on the Original Story by Loren Eiseley

This version is part of the Starthrower Foundation

One day a man was walking along the beach when he noticed a boy picking something up and gently throwing it into the ocean.

Approaching the boy, he asked, "What are you doing?"

The youth replied, "Throwing starfish back into the ocean. The surf is up, and the tide is going out. If I don't throw them back, they'll die."

"Son," the man said. "Don't you realize there are miles and miles of beach and hundreds of starfish? You can't make a difference."

After listening politely, the boy bent down, picked up another starfish, and threw it back into the surf. Then, smiling at the man, he said, **"I made a difference for that one."**

Are You Being a Difference Maker?

YOU HOLD IN YOUR hand the power to change a life, a mind, or circumstances. You have the power (with God's help) to change the life of at least one person. After escaping the fish, Jonah preached to the city of Nineveh, and the entire city repented. Can you find one young person, friend, neighbor, or street person for whom you can bring a moment of happiness?

A friend of mine prepared breakfast five days a week for a motherless boy living with his father who went to work very early. Each day on his way to school, this lad stopped for a quick fried egg, toast, juice, cereal, or whatever was available. Then my mothering friend would grab her own things and drop him off at high school. Was it a challenge and a bit of effort every day to have this added task? Absolutely. Did she make a difference in his life? You bet you she did. So "let your light shine before men, that they may see your good deeds, and praise your Father in heaven" (Matthew 5:16).

Sample Ideas to Tease Your Brain

- Know a lonely person who is celebrating a birthday? Grab a giant cupcake, stick a candle in the center, and surprise him/her with a cheery greeting and an off-key "Happy Birthday" melody.
- Is there a "home-alone" kid near you because family adults work? Why not plan a "Sit-on-the-Steps Party" and share a baloney sandwich or a taco, while discussing the latest ballgame scores? Maybe invite her to join you at church. You could be a difference maker in the life of that kiddo.
- Handy with a hammer? Use it to make a modest repair job for a shut-in, single mom, or stressed-out dad. Leave a little "God Loves You" card behind.
- Is your mower sharp and ready to roll? Eyeball a lawn in your neighborhood that looks a tad neglected. Go to work and then say, "Praise the Lord," if the owner comes out and says thanks.
- Have a few extra dollars? Ask a church youth minister if he has a student who would love to go on the summer youth outing but

lacks the funds. Then pray for growth and conviction for your love-offering recipient.

- Someone around you a bit sad? No family nearby? Perhaps even a bit timid? Go visit or take her a cup of tea. Sit and chat. Leave with a hug, quick prayer, and a giant smile. Didn't cost much, but perhaps you provided thirty minutes of smiles.

You were a difference maker.

So, my friends—maybe the time is right for you to begin throwing "starfish" back into the sea. Who needs your smile? Maybe a hug or a fresh strawberry? What about a rose, listening ear, or friendly companionship for lunch? Grab your keys and give a ride to the doctor for one without a car. Go out to a local senior center/care facility and ask the head desk person for the name of someone with no visitors. Just drop in and see if a smile will brighten his or her day.

**Be brave. Be bold. Make a difference for
the Lord's starfish, our friends.**

Awe

SEPTEMBER FOUND US ON the shores of Iceland. Chill, desolation, friendliness, geysers, bright flowers, wild blueberries, tourists, and mystical trolls created deep memories. As we viewed Gullfoss waterfalls, with God's promised rainbow arching over the scene, one could not help but draw a deep breath and stand in awe. For wildness and fury, it outdoes Niagara Falls. Surely this demands words of praise for our Creator.

Wonder

"The heavens declare the glory of God; the skies proclaim the work of his hands" (Psalm 19:1). This Icelandic lad's expression depicts pure joy as he explores a small seed.

I hope that each reader experiences at least one moment of wonder every day. Catch a glimpse of the clusters of orange and red leaves swishing in the breeze. Murmur a word of praise as you watch the white pelicans glide over the lake on their way to warmer winter weather. Gleefully gaze at the grandchild in your arms and say, "Thanks, God, for your creation."

Reflection

This kitten caught my eye as our tour group wandered down the Icelandic streets. Sitting quietly, she just watched the world go by. When I reviewed the photo later, I was stunned by what else was there: the reflection of the trees and building outside of the house. The lacy curtains almost covered up God's world. I had focused on the little furry feline. A second look was required to acknowledge God's creation.

Parade magazine of October 9, 2016, discussed the feeling of awe. Paula Scott shared a study suggesting that awe is a dramatic feeling with the power to inspire, heal, change our thinking, and bring people together. Researchers now think that awestruck is a basic part of being human. Each human needs to experience wonderment and awe. It is an experience of being a small part of something much larger. We shift our thinking from *me* to *we* or perhaps to *Thee*. Well, friends, God is responsible for much of that wonder. He created these breathtaking images of nature. *Parade* quoted one man's experience of awe: "Through backpacking and rock-climbing trips, I literally climbed out of depression." Do you need healing from depression, worry, stress, or loneliness? Recognize the power of awe. Open your eyes and recognize God's greatness.

Read scripture. Pause and reflect on His power and majesty. **Be in awe.** You, too, will experience the feeling of being in the presence of something vast and beyond human scale.

That is the wonder of God.

New World Record

FIFTY-EIGHT INDIAN ARMY PERSONNEL set a new world record in 2017 by riding a single motorcycle at the Indian Air Force base in Bengaluru. This group, known as the Tornadoes, rode a 500 cc Royal Enfield motorbike for twelve hundred meters, setting a record in the *Guinness Book of World Records*.

Imagine fifty-eight men smashed together, hanging onto a pair of support bars running the length of a little platform fastened onto the frame of the cycle. How they managed to attach the platform to a two-wheeler is amazing. Balance, cooperation, togetherness, teamwork, leadership, relationships, and trust are but a few of the words suggested by this demonstration. These close buddies depended on each other for support as this carrier tipped slightly from one side to the other while moving down the runway. (www.khaleejtimes.com/international/india/video-58-indian-army-men-set-new-world-recordride-on-single-motorcycle)

There are three key persons in the adventure. If viewing this spectacular event, you would see one head slightly higher than the rest. He is the "balancer," who stays on the top and ensures that each member of the team stays balanced. A slight movement by a team member could cause the entire group to become unbalanced, resulting in a catastrophe. Another key person, the "rider," controls the mechanical parts of the bike, such as the brakes. The third member of the trio is the "navigator," who becomes the eyes for the driver.

What about the Christian family? As we proceed through life, we often find ourselves attempting to avoid a crash. Day-to-day trials and problems collide with joys and blessings. We face a delicate balancing act. Are we going to crash or cruise forward? Wrapping our arms around each other with love and support may be just the factor keeping us from crashing, figuratively speaking.

Remember, there are three key elements of this fifty-eight-member biking team. Riding on the back, we have the Balancer. His eye constantly scans the team to make certain all members stay balanced. If one member gets out of whack, the entire cluster will crumble to the ground. Likewise in our Christian family. Guess who stands above, watching over our team to make certain we all stay aboard? The psalmist reminds us: "He [God] will not let your foot slip—he who watches over you will not slumber" (Psalm 121:3). We also read that, "The eyes of the Lord are on the righteous: and His ears are attentive to their cry" (Psalm 34:15). A song made famous by Ethel Waters echoes through my head: "I sing because I'm happy. I sing because I'm free. For His eye is on the sparrow, and I know He watches me." Yes, God is looking out for you as well as our feathered friends. He is our Balancer.

The rider actually controls the engine and workings of the vehicle. If our Christian team is going to move forward, we also must have workers who keep the engine running. The church needs many of these leaders. Tasks may include organizing calling teams or work groups, supervising greeters, teaching classes, encouraging missionaries far from home, or performing a multitude of other jobs. Leaders, the Kingdom needs you to keep moving forward. Accept your role. Jump aboard and provide that energy for the rest of the team.

Finally, the navigator is the eyes for the team. Yes, God watches over us, but each of us must also reach out to others. Help a friend avoid a bump in life. Find a college kid, new mom, or senior who needs a bit of guidance over the stumps in their path. Be proactive. Take your blinders off and reach out. Hop on with the team and help, using whatever gifts God has given you.

"As each has received a gift, employ it in serving one another,
as good managers of the grace of God in its
various forms" (1 Peter 4:10 RSV).
"Let each of you look not only to his own interests, but also
to the interests of others" (Philippians 2:4 RSV).

Help one person today, and give God the praise.

Death of the Thimble

MONOPOLY ICON VANISHES—THE THIMBLE. During the Great Depression (1935), we had the top hat, boot, iron, race car, a puppy, and the thimble. No more. Voters in a recent contest elected to dump the sewing icon, along with the wheelbarrow and boot. Following voting by 4.3 million fans, three new tokens replace those burned into our memories: a rubber ducky, penguin, and a T-Rex join the Scottie, top hat, roadster, cat, and battleship.

Our family spent many a rainy day enjoying the art of buying and selling imaginary properties. Today, I sometimes wistfully think, *What if I had initiated a real-estate gene in my body and actually bought and sold homes and lands?* Regardless, the thimble moved around the board bringing joy or sadness as the player bought, sold, and paid rent.

From the early 1940s to the 1960s, my mother frequently utilized the tiny finger protector. Today, that icon rests on my dresser. Times have changed, and premade clothes dominate our wardrobes. I cannot remember the day when I used the little item to help create or mend. Children today rarely have any idea regarding the original purpose of the thimble. Even sewing machines are rare household items. My mother had a portable machine that fit in a small carrying case about twice the size of an old-fashioned typewriter. We carried that item wherever we moved over the years. Even the leather handle was worn off. I must admit that my mother's daughter rarely used it. My niece in Alabama is the owner of that icon today.

As I read this story, however, another thought leaped into my brain. Staring at me from the corner of the Monopoly board was a giant word: GO. Regardless of what placeholder one used during the game, the challenge was to "go." That is exactly what the Christian's challenge remains today: GO. Jesus's command is loud and clear: "Go into all the world and preach the good news to all creation." Why? Because "whoever believes and is baptized will be saved, but whoever does not believe will be condemned" (Mark 16:15–16).

That command has not changed. No voting of Christ followers can change that order by Christ, the chief in charge. Where are we to go? Into all the world—far and wide—including our own backyards, challenging neighborhoods, areas of unrest as well as corners of peace. As we go, we must take His Word in our hearts and share it with love and compassion. Think today of just one person you know who needs a closer relationship with God. Then go. Go today. Go with love in your heart.

Just "go tell it on the mountain, that Jesus Christ is born."

Pregnant Teen Says Baby Is God's

Who would possibly believe her story? How would
the **Bethlehem Gazette** report the birth?
What thoughts could possibly wander through
the teen's head during her pregnancy?
How does a youthful mother prepare to deliver the Son of God?
With whom might she share the news first? Her
parents? Best friend? Fiancé? Cousin?
What question might you have asked this new mother prior to
the birth? Any advice you would have given a first-time mom?

WHEN WE APPROACH THE season of the year to remember and celebrate the birth of the Christ Child, take time also to reflect on Mary. We rightly focus on the birth of the Savior of the world, but for a few moments, let's focus on the mother of Jesus.

Mary came from a humble background, a small-town girl betrothed to a young carpenter of the village. We know very little about her except what is recorded in the scriptures. *Mary* means "wise woman" or "lady." Certainly, after being told by Gabriel that she would be the mother of the Son of God, it would take a wise mother to process that news. No wonder she journeyed to see her cousin Elizabeth, the mother of John the Baptist. They probably discussed many topics, including the special revelations they each had regarding their future sons. My imagination, however, assumes they also discussed proper childcare procedures which first-time mothers need.

I also wonder what the gossips of the day whispered about this unmarried young Galilean woman who was with child. The family must have been embarrassed, especially since they were to believe there was no human father. Her pregnancy would dishonor each of them in those days.

I understand from others' experiences that giving birth it generally a difficult process, even in twenty-first-century hospitals. Imagine a straw-filled manger for the delivery room in Bethlehem. Medical professionals were probably the father and an innkeeper as stand-ins. No way could my father have filled that role, as he was way too bashful and embarrassed in such situations. Some historians do suggest that a group of Mary's female relatives might have been present, acting as midwives.

Mary had to be one tough mama. The trio took off for Egypt soon after she gave birth. Riding on the back of a four-legged beast while trying to escape Herod's agents in pursuit of this alleged King of the Jews must have been backbreaking. No friendly motel left its lights on to welcome them. Where do you go for housing? One also wonders how quickly the young carpenter found work to support his family. And then while in Jerusalem on temple business, she loses her son. Panic time. Back to the city and wonder of wonders—there was the kid interacting with the leaders of the temple. Perhaps on the way home, she had a discussion with the twelve-year-old about sticking close to His parents. First-century Jewish Mary would conduct homeschooling. Could you have filled those sandals of this caretaker of Jesus?

Mothers today follow their offspring to every soccer game, band concert, or teacher conference. Mary followed her son also. Mark initially tells us about a crowd who clustered around Jesus, asking questions. Suddenly, the dialogue is interrupted as a messenger calls out, "Your mother and your brothers and sisters are outside, asking for you" (Mark 3:31–35). Or, it's party time and Mary joins Jesus at the wedding feast in Cana, even suggesting her son be thoughtful and provide wine for the hostess when a shortage arises. And of course, the most difficult moment of Jesus's earthly life: His crucifixion. Right at His feet, we find Mary. Her son acknowledges her presence and invites John to take care of her. I don't know about you, but remembering that action always fills my heart with sadness, but also joy, that even in such severe pain, Jesus took care of Mom.

Take a few moments and ponder some of the questions listed above. Mary was given a special opportunity to give birth to the Son of God. Each of us has unique abilities and talents we must use in His service. Jesus Christ is still Immanuel: God with us.

**Let us hop on our donkey and go forth to witness,
until this Christ Child returns as victorious King
to take us home to be with Him forever.**

Burn Out or Just Burn?

What about You?

ARE YOU RUNNING ON empty? Each morning as you drag yourself out of bed, does your mind say, "Yuk! Another day? Just give me a cave in which to crawl and I'll hibernate until the June bugs arrive"? Elijah must have been experiencing some of those thoughts. After he successfully challenged eight hundred and fifty pagan priests of Baal to match wits and power with him, he was in the depths of fatigue. Drought had ravaged the country. With the power of the living God, however, Elijah's sacrifice was immediately consumed by fire. The prophets of Baal were killed, and God sent rain. But then an unexpected thing happened. Elijah ran for his life to avoid the wrath of Jezebel. In 1 Kings 18, we read of the challenge between the Baal prophets and our hero, but chapter 19 is even more amazing and meaningful for today.

Elijah was frightened. He was probably mentally exhausted and discouraged, even though he had just witnessed two great spiritual victories: the defeat of prophets of Baal and end of the drought. He ran to Beersheba and then another day into the wilderness. He sat down by a bush and prayed to die. "I've had enough, Lord. Take my life" (1 Kings 19:4). He then went to sleep. Some time later, an angel woke him and ordered him to eat. Snack time and another nap. Again, the angel woke him and told him to eat, after which he traveled for another forty days. That is quite a little hike—forty days. I'm tired after one afternoon of hiking.

The voice of the Lord inquired as to what Elijah was doing. "I've been very zealous for the Lord God Almighty" (1 Kings 19:10). Our guy Elijah really thought he was the only one left loving God. Another command came from the Lord: "Go out and stand on the mountain," and wait for me (1 Kings 19:11). You must read the details for yourself, but bottom line, Elijah was told to return home and do work for the Lord.

Perhaps we who become weary, sad, lonely, disgusted, disappointed, or even a little mad at God can learn from Elijah's life. What did God do to lead him out of his depression? First, God let him rest and eat. Then God confronted him and challenged him to return to his mission, to his work of speaking out on behalf of God. Get yourself back in gear. Return to the battle.

When you are maxed out emotionally from family, work, church volunteering, or even just worshipping, listen to God. Find time for rest. No more burning the midnight oil or candle at both ends. Forget the diet or fasting. Eat healthy foods: fruit, vegetables, and maybe even sneak in a little pizza. Then comes the tough part. Rearm yourself with the spiritual armor of God (Ephesians 6:10–18). Climb back on your skateboard and complete your responsibilities. Get the job done. Stay on focus. Your unique skills and talents are needed by God and your family, spouse, church, or community. You cannot run away and hide.

Burnout is truly a challenge for many loyal, hardworking Christians, including our ministers and staff. We want to quit. That is not an option in God's eyes. We are to be faithful to the end. We are to burn for God, not **burn out**. Paul reminded Timothy to "fan into flame the gift of God, which is in you" (2 Timothy 1:6). Sometimes it appears that we, as happened to Elijah, run on empty after completing an extraordinary event, job, or duty. We have experienced the high and then fall apart after the wedding, our surgery, the sermon, caregiving responsibilities, or seeing the children off to school. Periods of stress wear one out. Even the daily grind can produce burnout. Remember God's formula: Rest. Eat. Return to the job.

Get the fire kindled again and burn for the Lord. The early Christians were ablaze with God's spirit. You, too, can burn for the Lord until death does call.

Reflections from the Big Apple

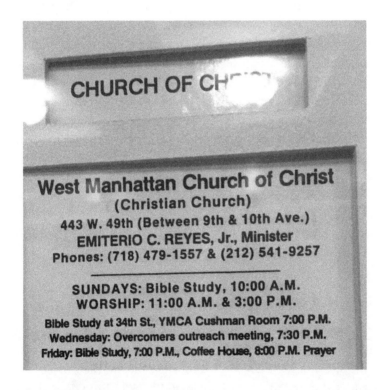

CHURCH OF CHRIST

West Manhattan Church of Christ
(Christian Church)
443 W. 49th (Between 9th & 10th Ave.)
EMITERIO C. REYES, Jr., Minister
Phones: (718) 479-1557 & (212) 541-9257

SUNDAYS: Bible Study, 10:00 A.M.
WORSHIP: 11:00 A.M. & 3:00 P.M.
Bible Study at 34th St., YMCA Cushman Room 7:00 P.M.
Wednesday: Overcomers outreach meeting, 7:30 P.M.
Friday: Bible Study, 7:00 P.M., Coffee House, 8:00 P.M. Prayer

A TRIP TO NEW York City is filled with excitement, wonder, screeching sirens, pushcarts, jammed sidewalks, rip-off purse vendors, and comic entertainers. The constant cacophony of the city drives you crazy until your ears become dull to the hawkers, honkers, and hustlers. While in bed one midnight, the silence was shattered by parade drums and related instruments. Why a midnight band? No idea.

We sailed around the Statue of Liberty, tromped through the Metropolitan Museum of Art, and enjoyed numerous Broadway plays. A man on two crutches struggled to dodge the cabs and foot traffic as he moved through construction on Times Square. My mind did a mini-prayer: *Thanks, Lord, for two feet on which to walk.*

The subway system beats cabs and buses, but even they are crammed with sadness and defeat. Exiting one subway car, I saw an older man in a motorized wheelchair approach the open door. He managed to get the front two wheels into the car, but no way would the back wheels move forward. As the doors began to close, I grabbed the handles of the wheelchair and dragged him inside. We so need to keep our eyes open for ways to help those who struggle. Again, a prayer of thanksgiving.

Begging always makes me uncomfortable. A mother with a child and a collection cup brings tears to my eyes. The most distressing sight, however, was a man obviously seriously ill, lying on a pallet under a bit of a construction overhang on a Broadway sidewalk. Surrounding him were a few personal belongings, a bit of water in a cracked bowl, and food bits. Attending him was a young lady wiping his face with a damp cloth. He appeared homeless and incapacitated. I just wanted Jesus to drop by and say, "Take up your bed and walk."

The one flickering light of hope in this city of 24/7 dazzle and sparkle was the small group of Christians meeting weekly in a small room on Forty-Ninth Street. For several years now, I wander several blocks from my hotel to join this faithful band of believers and share the Lord's Supper, prayer, and preaching. Thirteen of us sang as the piano player kept us in tune. Friendliness filled the air. Acceptance of all, including street people, was evident. That day, one elderly man slipped in, dressed with bright-lime tennis shoes, faded green pants, grubby jacket hanging loose on his shoulders, and a dirty ball cap slammed on his head. I believe he entered from the street at least ten times and exited before the service was over. He wandered over to the snack table and back out the door. The group knew him. His life had been filled with drugs, and ruin was the result. Never once did the speaker pause as the interruptions continued. Folks were accepting.

I know not what lives have been touched by this faithful few, but I know Christ is living with them and helping them minister to the poor, hungry, and ailing. Perhaps we need to pray for this congregation of believers who preach the Word. That day they indicated the collection box needed a thousand dollars to bring them back into the black. I wished my checkbook had been in my pocket as I dropped a few bills into the box on the table.

Wonder wandered through my brain during the week in the Big Apple. Who is helping these invisible folks in need? We all just walk by and ignore their presence. How many children are sleeping by garbage cans and seeking handouts? What happened to politeness? Just holding the door for someone seemed like a lost art. Then the words *empathy* and *love* flashed before my eyes. Have we replaced caring for others with self-indulgence? Are we unable to appreciate others and care for those with special challenges? Are we, as citizens of this world today, more eager to fulfill our own goals and ignore the sick, the lame, the blind, the senior, or the homeless? Do we expect the government to provide for the needs of the crippled and hungry as we gulp down our Happy Meal or cherry-tomato pizza? Who have I helped along the way this day, week, or lifetime?

Matthew 25:35 suggests we show our love when we feed the hungry and clothe the naked. Proverbs 19:17 reminds the reader that "whoever is generous to the poor lends to the Lord, and he will repay him for his deed." We are told to give a cup of cold water to the thirsty in His name (Matthew 10:42). Solomon in Proverbs 22:9 claims, "Whoever has a bountiful eye will be blessed, for he shares his bread with the poor." Here's a tougher proverb: "Honor the Lord with your wealth and with the first fruits of all your produce" (Proverbs 3:9). It appears Christians need to reach out with smiles, love, gifts of graciousness, and sharing in a sacrificial way.

Michelle Borba in *Time* magazine (June 6, 2016) has a word for our serious empathy deficit. She calls it the "Selfie Syndrome." Borba attributes it to the rise of social media, especially among our youth. I, for one, am ready to prove her wrong.

Help me, as together we open our eyes to see the needs of the hurting. Open our hearts to care. Open our pocketbooks to share. Share our time, energy, possessions, and most importantly, share our love of Christ.

**He came for everyone: rich, poor, ill, lame,
druggie, and yes, even for you and me.**

What an Upside-Down World

Sloths are furry, slow-moving animals. They spend
most of their time hanging upside down high in the
forest canopy, feeding on leaves and resting.

ACTUALLY, SLOTHS COME DOWN to earth only to excrete waste or to
move to a different area. They can take up to a month to digest a single
meal. Sloths have just cheek teeth. Imagine hanging by your feet so much
of your life. When on the ground, they move only about fifty-three feet per
hour. While in trees, they can travel about 480 feet per hour. They spend
most of their day resting and sleeping, and at night, they find food to eat.
They truly live upside down.

Our two-toed friend reminded me of Paul and Silas as they entered
Thessalonica. They had just made a midnight escape from prison in

Philippi after God caused an earthquake to break open the prison doors. The jailer was ready to insert a sword into himself when Paul yelled out, "Stop!" Right on the spot, he heard a mini-sermon by Preacher Paul resulting in many lives being changed for good. The next day, they were asked to leave town by the city fathers, and off to Thessalonica they trotted (Acts 16:11–40).

Life in the new city also proved difficult. You just can't keep a God-driven guy down. Paul went public again. For three weeks he preached in the synagogue. In fact, he even argued with the synagogue staff. You guessed it. In trouble again for not keeping quiet. The Jews were jealous because of the many followers of our "crazy" friend. These Jewish leaders attacked the house of Jason hoping to find his houseguest Paul.

When they couldn't find Paul, they dragged Jason and some others before the city officials. A heated discussion followed. The accusation they made was, "These men who have turned the world upside down have come here also" (Acts 17:6 RSV). What a crime! Paul had made such an impression on the community in twenty-one days that they wanted him out. Hanging out in their town was upsetting the in crowd of leaders. Paul immediately had to sail away to Athens, and again, what does he do? Preaches, witnesses to strangers, and shares the gospel in the synagogue. He continued to turn the world upside down. Ridiculed, opposed, and persecuted, but he just continued with boldness.

Zacchaeus, a rather short fellow, climbed into a tree to see and hear the Master as He came along the parade route. Jesus knew Mr. Z. was there and told him to get out of the tree: "Come down! I want to have lunch with you and a little chat." They had never met. As he was a tax collector, Zacchaeus had few friends. And yet, wonder of wonders, with whom did Jesus select to have a personal conversation? This outcast, everyday working stiff (Luke 19:1–10). He was required, however, to get down off his limb to be selected for service with the Master.

Two messages seem to surface from our stories. One, God requires us to turn the world upside down. We must be bold. There are people who make waves and upset the system. There are Christians who disturb the peace and the comfort of sinners. The second message suggests, however, that we have to get out of the tree and go find those needing God's love, care, and forgiveness. Watching from the sidelines does not work. We must be engaged in the spreading a healing balm for a hurting world.

You, too, must help turn the world upside down—your world at South Ash, Falling Brook, Little Rock, or Jane's Family Snack Shop. Be bold.

Some folks don't know what's happening.
Some folks watch things happen.
Others make things happen. Which are you?

Our Creator Does Big Things. Not All Trees Have a Nickname, But the President Has Earned One

A GIANT SEQUOIA STANDS 247 feet tall and is estimated to be over thirty-two hundred years old. It was discovered in 1869 and was named after President McKinley following his assassination in 1901. For all these years, no loggers took it down, nor did any forest fire or earthquake topple it. Imagine, this tree was already twelve hundred years old when Jesus walked the earth. A visit to Sequoia National Park will provide you with a view of this record breaking redwood tree.

The trunk of the President measures at twenty-seven feet across, with two billion needles from base to top. Because of its size, this tree had never been photographed in its entirety until recently. A team of *National Geographic* photographers worked with scientists to try and create the first photo of the entire tree.

Photographers climbed the tree with pulleys and levers to take thousands of photos. They then selected one hundred twenty-six and stitched them together to get an incredible picture. Perhaps you can even imagine seeing one tiny spot near the top. That would be a man, no larger than a small dot.

"When I consider your heavens, the work of your fingers, the moon and the stars, which you have ordained, what is man that you are mindful of him, and the son of man that you visit him" (Psalm 8:3–4). God created everything. He created the blue whale: two hundred tons of blubber. The hog-nosed bat (bumblebee bat) is no longer than the end of your finger. Sultan Kosen from Turkey was eight feet, three inches tall and weighed 485 pounds at time of his death. Records suggest that there are about four hundred thousand flowering plant species in our world. Creation is truly an extravagant gesture by God.

And then, wonders of wonders, He created you. You with eyes that have automatic focus. You with ears that capture sound waves out of the air, translate them into vibrations, and send those signals to the brain to be interpreted. It takes quite a Creator to create humans in His own image. Did you stop and say, "Thank you, God," for His greatness?

And then, one last demonstration of His power: His Son rose from the dead. And yes, don't forget to tell your friends. His death and resurrection is the power behind our opportunity to likewise someday be raised from the grave to be with Him.

He is one big God.

Unexpected Love

FEBRUARY 14 ARRIVES EVERY year. Mounds of greeting cards, both paper and electronic, will be generated, expressing our love for a friend, family member, or maybe even for someone we hardly know. Chocolates, red tulips, and fancy dinners will delight others on this day set aside to show our appreciation and love.

A few folks will be lonely. Empty mailbox for others. For some, dinner of Frosted Flakes will be without candles or a companion. Leftover Christmas candy and wilting poinsettia may supply the calories and decorations for the special evening identified for love for singles in an empty apartment. Love is essential for emotional and physically sound health. Hurting folks need a large dose of love.

The wonderful news we need to share with all is that love is available to anyone, to anyone reaching out to Christ. Sometimes, folks recognize this gift quite unexpectedly. Remember the Good Samaritan? Some guy is bleeding along the road to Jericho after thugs beat and rob him. Think what was going on in his mind: Worry. Pain. Concern for his family. *Will anyone stop and care for me?* Despair clouds his thinking. He is alone and feeling unloved. Where is his caring neighbor?

Suddenly, through half-opened eyes, he spots a priest walking toward him, perhaps a leader from his temple. Hope leaps within his mind. And then, with sinking heart, he sees the priest ignore him. A few moments later, as he hangs on to life, he notices a Levite looking down at him. Oh, boy. Help at last—but no. This religious leader just journeys on with nary a word of comfort or a Band-Aid to halt the bleeding.

Fear grips his heart. Maybe he sends up a tiny prayer, asking God for forgiveness for himself. Perhaps it's a prayer for peace for his family when they discover his beaten body. As he curls up in pain, footsteps once again are heard. By now, however, he has given up on rescue. Nobody will take time from their busy schedule to help him. But what? What is this? *I feel someone touching me and applying soothing ointment to my wounds. Who is this? A Samaritan? We Jews hate them. We treat them with disdain. Surely he is not going to help me, but … Oh, my! He just lifted me up on his donkey, and off we go to the local motel. My needs were taken care of by the most unexpected person: a hated Samaritan.*

Jesus told this little story after being asked, "What must I do to inherit eternal life?" followed by "Who is my neighbor?" Jesus replied, "Thou shalt love the Lord thy God with all thy heart, and with all thy soul and with all thy mind, and thy neighbor as thyself." He then defines our neighbor with the "Good Samaritan" account in Luke 10:25–37. Sometimes the most unexpected, hated individual surprises us with love and concern. Are we ready to accept care and concern from an individual on the wrong side of the tracks or from a country with whom we might be at war? Alternately, are we prepared to demonstrate love, including action, toward the kid with a different skin color, a dad who spent time in jail, or an angry neighbor who just ran over your dogwood tree with his pickup truck? Sharing and showing love may take courage.

In 1 Corinthians 13:1–7, we read that true love is kind and patient, never fails, does not exhibit ego problems or put itself first. This is unexpected. When Naaman, the Syrian general, was suffering from leprosy, he received help from a most unexpected friend. His wife's servant girl, whom he had captured in Israel, taken away from her family, and made a slave, contacted the prophet Elisha (2 Kings 5:1–16). The prophet provided miraculous healing for the general. Love came from an unexpected source.

What about you? Are you remembering that God so loved the world that He gave His only Son for anyone who believes in Him (John 3:16)? Yes. You, a sinner. Can you imagine you giving your life for someone who has messed up her life? Sure, occasionally it happens, but Christ did it for every single sinner in the world who will recognize His love, acknowledge His forgiveness, and change his or her life.

God's love is unexpected.
Today's challenge: Share this news with friends.
They, too, need to experience unexpected love.

Ready for Action

**Beginner in a UTV speeding along. Anxious? Yes.
Uncertain? Of course. Hopeful? Great anticipation.**

FOLKS WERE GATHERING IN the waiting area adjacent to our cruise liner in anticipation of an afternoon adventure. A pair of tour employees were checking us in. As we watched them, they whispered and took quick looks in our direction. My heart beat a bit faster. Had we made the right decision for our trip?

My friend had been a bit reluctant when I suggested this three-hour, motorized tour of the island of Aruba. Six other couples had arrived, each probably in their thirties or forties. What were two eighty-plus-year-old females doing here, anyway? Boarding the bus scheduled to deliver us to the beginning of our wild journey, my heart began to pound just a bit. Could we really handle the challenge? What difficulties would we experience? Warnings on the information reminded drivers not to exceed forty miles per hour, always follow the guide precisely, go directly down a steep incline as vehicles tip over easily. Wow! Was this really that dangerous? We received papers to sign relieving the company of all responsibility for our safety or death. Oh, me! Although I said nothing aloud, I sent a tiny prayer for protection heavenward.

Following a brief lecture and review of the guidelines, we found our assigned ultra-light terrain vehicle (UTV), boarded, and started our engines with a roar. These four-wheelers took off like a shot. Our parade of eight off-road carts whizzed down the city streets bustling with traffic, around four traffic circles, and through several curves. Clutching the steering wheel as if it would jump out of my hands, I began to relax a bit. Yes. Maybe I could manage this monster and keep us safe. My attitude began to change. I can do this. If these forty-year-old men can streak across the rocks and curves, so can I—and we did. Joy began to fill my heart.

Suddenly, the terrain changed. An unpaved, crooked, rocky trail demanded shifting to four-wheel drive. The simple tube of stretchy cloth given to us made sense. Insert head. Pull up over hair and nose to protect self from whirling dust. We had arrived. My heart thumped once more as we passed over rocks large enough to knock holes in the underbody of the UTV. Stopping only occasionally to view the ocean, an ancient gold mine, and an old church, one hundred eighty minutes flew by. It was time to return to the safety of our floating home. Our young travel companions expressed surprise and maybe a bit of admiration that the old ladies kept up. This trip will remain long in my memory. New experiences bring both fear and joy. Action is exciting. We must stay young in spirit.

As I reflect today, I think of Moses and the Children of Israel. They lived comfortably in Egypt after finding brother Joseph in charge of much of the kingdom during a time of drought in their homeland. They had food, shelter, and protection. Life continued as normal—day after boring day. Then, a new king arrived who knew not Joseph. Life changed. The Egyptians made their lives "bitter with hard labor in brick and mortar and with all kinds of work in the fields." They used them ruthlessly. Moses was born. Bingo! God saved him from Pharaoh's "slaughter-of-babies" order. God even found Moses a stepmother: none other than Pharaoh's daughter. Moses grew, made mistakes, married, and matured. God had a long-range task for him.

Now, the story shifts. God tells Moses to lead his people out of slavery and misery. Take them to the wilderness. Moses must suddenly lead about six hundred thousand men plus women and children into unknown territory. For 430 years, Egypt had been their home. What a night that must have been as Moses started out with the family. Do you suppose he might have been a bit frightened? Could his heart have been beating at a rapid pace when he raised his staff in front of the Red Sea, with the armies of Pharaoh racing toward him? Of course, his heart beat too rapidly. But what did he do? God told him not to be afraid. He trusted God. He took action, and the sea parted. His family was safe. Life was good. Perhaps Moses slept better that night. Now he just needed to begin a forty-year walk in the wilderness.

So you, too, my friend, must step out. Whether you have gray hair, pretend dark hair, or minus hair on your head, it is no excuse not to engage in new adventures. The Lord wants workers in His vineyard. Look for new areas of outreach for the Kingdom. Ask for a new task at church. Reach out to a neighbor in need. Volunteer for something different. Yes, there will be a bit of fear, nervousness, or sleeplessness.

But the blessing and joy of sharpening new skills will keep you alert and bring joy to you and to the Lord.

Christmas Reflections

Memories from Childhood

CHRISTMAS WAS A SPECIAL time at our home when I was a child. Life was simple. A tromp in the woods with our ax would produce a Missouri cedar tree. Carefully, my little brother and I would hang silver icicles, one by one (never a clump thrown casually). A few strings of lights topped with an angel completed our efforts. It brightened our small home for two or three weeks, until the needles fell on the floor, making a wonderful fire hazard.

"Stockings were hung by the chimney with care." Christmas morning, our parents watched as John and I peeked into the socks. Santa left candy, an orange, and some other small items. We eagerly emptied the loot. Breakfast was special—the only tradition I can remember our family ever had: fried cornmeal mush. Oh, that was such a treat. Even today, part of my family helps me relive that memory. I do believe I am the only one thrilled with crunchy, greasy, fried cornmeal, but families care for each other, and so, out comes the annual fried mush and maple syrup. I am given the honor of frying it crispy thin. Annually, my mind replays seventy-five or so years of history as I flip the yummy morsels in the pan.

Each of the presents were wrapped with love. Gifts were small. One year, my brother and I pooled our money, went to the hardware store, and returned with a small paring knife for my mom. Mothers are blessed with the ability to appear thrilled at the most insignificant, unglamorous item. I don't know if we even had money for a gift for our father. (I guess Dads have to be tough.) A small package would arrive from our maternal grandmother each year. Unwrapping the brown paper, we would uncover her acts of love. Every year, there was a small parcel of dried corn used for soup and a package of dried fruit from their farm. That was it, but we loved the taste of food prepared with care by her gnarly little fingers. My grandmother was always old, gray-haired, stooped, and wrinkled, at least in my memory.

The Christmas story was read. Sometimes small images from a manger scene would be used, along with the oral tradition for visual effect. Although Santa came to our home, Christ was certainly key to the celebration of the day.

If my memory serves me correctly, we never shared the day with any family member other than the four of us. Our grandparents lived in Oregon and Washington. Vacation time was short. Money was even shorter, so driving or flying was an impossible dream. I wonder now as I mature, how much my mother must have missed never sharing the glorious day with her family after her marriage.

As we close this rather personal reflection, let's take a moment to remember the gifts given by the most generous giver of all givers: God himself. He is a giver, not a taker. James 1:17 tells us, "God is the giver of every good and perfect gift." In Acts 17:25, we read that God "gives all men life and breath." Daily He supplies us with air, water, health, love, and hope. He gave a lavish gift—the gift of His very only Son, Christ. "For to us a child is born, to us a son is given, and the government will be on his shoulders. And he will be called Wonderful Counselor, Mighty God, Everlasting Father, Prince of Peace" (Isaiah 9:6). He also works through His children (Christians) who in turn shower others with friendship, love, compassion, and support in times of need.

Paul reminds us in Acts 20:35 that it is "more blessed [makes one happier] to give than to receive." As a small child, that is certainly a difficult concept, but today, as an adult, I cherish the opportunity to share with others. God delights seeing His people gladly providing for the needs of His church and His children.

During December, our communities and churches reach out with snow boots, mittens, toy trucks, turkeys, and baskets of goodies. That is to be commended, but let's rewire. Think twelve months of sharing. Families need lights, heat, peanut butter, diapers, sandals, and loving 365 days of a year. Discuss with your family the challenge of adopting a secret cause for one entire year. Plot strategy for caring in a silent manner. Encourage your children to share a portion of their allowance or earnings with this secret family. Budget wisely as a family. Give, and then praise the Lord for His generosity to your family, which allows you the privilege of sharing with others. Together with the Lord, all things are possible.

I have my secret adopted family for the new year. Join me. Find your place to help. Whether single, retired, youthful, rich, or financially challenged, reach out in love. Your gift may be actions of helpfulness rather than dollar bills or snow cones.

That is okay. You are giving, and God rejoices.

Big Sun, No Sun, His Son

Without the sun, we would be nothing.
No vegetation, no life, no you.
With the sun, we have warmth, light, growth, health, and sunburn.

From the time of creation, God said, "Let there be
light, and there was light" (Genesis 1:3).
God is happy about that. We are happy about that.
God created the moon and separated the light from darkness.
God called the light "day," and the darkness He called "night."
God was happy about that.
Lovers, dreamers, and hoot owls rejoice.
New adventures happen as the world whirls around.
The moon, the earth, and the sun rearrange themselves constantly.
Occasionally, wonderful results appear,
a total solar eclipse: wow.

On Monday, August 21, 2017, beginning at 11:25 a.m., in Springfield,
folks were able to grab special solar glasses
and observe an almost total eclipse.
The maximum blocking of the sun's rays in
this area occurred at 1:18 p.m.
Most of the sun was blocked by our moon. Some even saw stars.
Really, no sun for us?

Just stop and think, my friends. Our God has created such
a marvelous, predictable world that scientists can announce
the exact minute and second for this solar excitement.

The enormity of our creation continues to
amaze and baffle this writer.
The precision of our universe far exceeds the accuracy of the
most marvelously human-made electronic instruments.
God knew what He was doing. Without this
sun, there would be no world.

Now stop and think.
Without God's other Son, where would we be? In deep, deep trouble.
He gave us His Son for our salvation.
No special glasses are needed to view Him.
He will live with us daily.
Are you as excited about His Son as the sun?
If not, why not?

"For God so loved the world that he gave us
His only begotten son" (John 3:16).

Latrine Duty Yes, Sir

FROM CINEMA TO MARRIOTT Hotel to former Carpet Barn, to old DHL Express Warehouse at the airport, and finally to Bob's Discount Furniture Store. A church on the move. What a story.

The headline story of the August 2017 issue of *Christian Standard* featured the East Point Christian Church in South Portland, Maine. Why, you ask, would that catch my attention? About twelve years before, folks from South Side Christian Church in Springfield, Illinois, helped in the birthing of Kingdom work in Maine.

Scott Taube, then minister at Fairfield Christian Church in Lancaster, Ohio, received a challenge to bring his family to Portland and begin a new congregation of believers. Portland, a city of 250,000 in a state of 1.3 million, had not one Restoration Movement church. After much prayer and discussion, the family journeyed northeast to begin a new life.

An old movie theater was located as a site for services but needed much attention. The help call went out. Jeff Chitwood, then minister at South Side, took a quartet of guys out to help ready the building. A few weeks later, a second group flew out to lend a hand. What a joyful experience for us. This writer remembers walking into the building and thinking, *Whoopee! There is much work to be done.*

Along with several others, I was assigned the job of making the bathrooms sparkle. Now imagine an old movie theater with thousands of bodies moving in and out of the restrooms over time. There was nothing pretty—just grit, grime, and glop. Our team immediately set out for the hardware store to acquire appropriate cleaning supplies. Returning to our station, we began to rub, scrub, and mumble. No progress was being made. Repeated trips to the hardware store allowed us to try every cleaning trick known to professional cleaners. After two days, the rooms remained dim and dull but slightly less repulsive. Latrine duty was over, but the memories remain.

Thank goodness other teams were more successful in their assignments, as they polished chairs or worked on the electrical and sound systems. We returned to Illinois, leaving fingerprints of love on this new worship center.

More than a dozen years have slipped by. The church has grown from a faithful handful to nearly two thousand, praising the Lord on Sunday mornings. Change of locations, however, became a habit. After about a month in the theater, mold was discovered, and the meeting place was moved to a Marriott Hotel. Space hampered, the congregation expanded to a former Carpet Barn and then to an old DHL Express Warehouse located adjacent to an airport. Think about those sounds during communion time.

Finally, growing attendance required a new site. Overcoming mounting obstacles, the group made their fifth move to a giant, remodeled former 92,000-square-foot big-box store. It includes an auditorium, indoor soccer field, classrooms, and a hundred-seat cafe. The sixteen-hundred-seat auditorium allows room for growth. Praise the Lord. And to think folks here in Springfield had a teeny-tiny part in the history of this dynamic assembly of worshipers.

Mission work is a part of South Side's DNA. Recently, teams flew to the Dominican Republic and to New York State to assist Christians needing worker bees to help forward movement. Literally getting our hands dirty on behalf of the Lord is a wonderful, wonderful feeling. If you ever have a chance to go, please go and serve. But also look for a place to serve with your home congregation.

My desire now is to once again visit Scott Taube and worship with the Portland Christians, the largest church of any kind in the state of Maine. Perhaps you, too, may crave an opportunity to visit this vibrant, growing group of believers. So pack up your duds, stuff the family in your car, and zip off to 345 Clarks Pond Parkway, South Portland, Maine. Surprise Scott and his wife, Beth. Tell them you heard about them from "Kathy, the latrine cleaning expert." I know you will be welcomed and receive a true blessing.

Hopefully you, too, are ready to share your talents to help the Kingdom expand. May I suggest you just open up your heart and glance around? You will find a need for your unique talents and energy.

Perhaps you, too, can become a latrine queen for the King.

His Royal Chair Is Not Vacant;
God Is on His Throne

"The twenty-four elders fall down before him who sits on the throne,
and worship him who lives for ever and ever. They lay their crowns
before the throne and say: **You are worthy, our Lord and God, to
receive glory and honor and power,** for you created all things, and by
your will they were created and have their being." (Revelation 4:10–11)

EZEKIEL, A PRIEST OF God, living in Jerusalem, was captured and taken
to Babylon. During his captivity, he had a vision of God. God appeared in
the midst of a tremendous storm filled with flashing lightning and fire. The
first chapter of Ezekiel explores the vision, concluding with this wonderful
description: "Above the expanse over their heads was what looked like a
throne of sapphire, and high above on the throne was a figure like that of
a man. I saw that from what appeared to be his waist up he looked like
glowing metal, as if full of fire, and that from there down he looked like
fire; and brilliant light surrounded him. Like the appearance of a rainbow
in the clouds on a rainy day, so was the radiance around him. This was
the appearance of the likeness of the glory of the Lord. When I saw it, I
fell facedown, and I heard the voice of one speaking" (Ezekiel 1:26–28).

God appeared on His throne. Ezekiel was given a job to do: to look up
the rebellious Israelite people and challenge them to return to God. God
was so upset with His children that He even called them obstinate and
stubborn (He was r-e-a-l-l-y upset).

God warned his servant Ezekiel that the job would be tough. In fact,
He said, "They may not even listen to you, but do the job anyway. Don't

be afraid—just preach away. You are my Watchman to warn and encourage my people."

The task was not a jolly good one. In fact, I would never apply for the job but would rather stay home, twiddling my thumbs. Nevertheless, the King has spoken, and we must obey. This King is everlasting, eternal, and waiting for His children to arrive at this glorious home. He is worthy to receive glory and honor from His servants. If you are a believer or follower, you are one of those servants.

John tells us in Revelation more about our king and his throne "I saw the Holy City, the new Jerusalem, coming down out of heaven from God, prepared as a bride beautifully dressed for her husband. And I heard a loud voice from the throne saying, Now the dwelling of God is with men, and he will dwell with them. They will be his people, and God himself will be with them and be their God. He will wipe every tear from their eyes. There will be no more death or mourning or crying or pain, for the old order of things has passed away" (Revelation 21:2–4).

What lessons might we take from these passages of scripture? There are at least six:

1. We are created by God.
2. We are to worship and bow down to him forever. Yes, even today.
3. God was, is, and will be on His throne. Praise the Lord.
4. His people are watchmen reaching out to folks, warning and encouraging, despite possible personal danger.
5. There will be a New Jerusalem, heaven, with no tears, or sickness, or sadness.
6. The throne is the center of attention with God, where we will receive mercy and find grace (Hebrews 4:1)

**Our Monarch reigns, rules, and remains
forever, waiting for our arrival.**

Sauerkraut and God, Part I

WHILE EATING A SALAD one day, I had an amazing experience. Chomping down on the normal lettuce, green onions, bacon bits, summer sausage, flakes of sharp cheese, and red pepper pieces, my tongue suddenly danced within my mouth. What was that unexpected taste? Was it to be savored or quickly spit out? Should I rejoice or worry that something harmful had been slipped into the greens?

Fortunately, my taste buds rewarded me with pleasure as I realized that something unexpected happened. Who in the world ever heard of mixing leftover chilled sauerkraut with cooked apple slices into the family salad? Apparently, the time had arrived to clean out the refrigerator, and into the mix went sauerkraut, along with sweet honey dressing.

The combination was strong and crunchy, but when blended in with the ordinary salad mix, the results were remarkable.

Could that also be true in our Christian lives? Does God occasionally wake up our complacency with an unanticipated challenge, experience, friend, or thought? Are there biblical examples of sauerkraut events? If yes, what were the results?

Remember Pharaoh's daughter? Just an ordinary day bathing in the Nile, and what a surprise: Floating in a basket was the future leader of the Children of Israel, crying his little eyes out. Did she scream? Run? Nope. She had compassion and adjusted her actions. Moses ultimately became her stepson and grew up in the palace environment. God knew who would act appropriately with this taste of the unexpected (Exodus 2:1–10).

Four guys were throwing their nets into the Sea of Galilee, anticipating a huge day's catch of squishy, smelly fish. Suddenly, some fellow on the shore interrupts their actions and offers them a challenge: "Come, follow me" (Matthew 4:20). Their sauerkraut moment: What in the world was this all about? Should we keep fishing or do the unexpected and follow Him? Yes, they dropped their nets and took off. Their lives were changed forever. God was in charge.

Other folks also experienced the unexpected. Mary, the mother of Jesus, certainly must have been startled when the angel told her she would be "found with child through the Holy Spirit" (Matthew 1:18–19). The world of Joseph and Mary was turned upside down because God interrupted their routine.

The little tax guy from Jericho who hung out in a sycamore-fig tree to view the passing dignitary (Jesus) must have been shocked when the group stopped under his tree. Rarely does the key figure in a parade challenge one of the participants. Zacchaeus was ordered down out of the tree and told to entertain Jesus. Wow! What an unexpected turn of events. Wonder what went through Mr. Z.'s head? *Did I make the bed before I left home? Do I have any refreshments to feed my guests?* Nevertheless, home they went, and Jesus shared wonderful news: "Today salvation has come to this house.... For the Son of Man came to seek and to save what was lost" (Luke 19:1–9). Mr. Z. initiated complete change of behavior, including giving 50 percent of his possessions to the poor.

The joy that Pharaoh's daughter, Mary, the four fishermen, and Zacchaeus experienced blended right in with their everyday existence, just like my salad. However, the flavor of their lives was enhanced by accepting the unexpected. Each must have continued their ordinary tasks (except the four fishermen) but with new focus. New purpose and value was added to their lives. The Master needed each, in some unique way, and they accepted the challenge.

So, dear reader, what about your life? Are your eyes open to a special calling from the Lord for your talents? Do you have the courage to accept that opportunity to serve, witness, care, or reach out in the name of the Lord? Will your family remember you for taking the unexpected step and challenge to help another? No, none of us will probably ever have quite such a sauerkraut moment in our lives as our four examples. However, even the widow became a sermon topic, as she dropped her mite into the collection box (Mark 12:38–44). Make your mite memorable.

Expect the unexpected. Look for the tingling opportunity to make a difference. Make certain you don't let age, fatigue, boredom, indifference, or self-centeredness crowd your brain, leaving no opportunity for experiencing the unanticipated.

Prepare for the unpredictable.
Don't be surprised when God reaches
out to catch your attention.
Just be ready to accept it. Go for it. Enjoy it.

Sauerkraut and God, Part II

IN PART I, I shared my surprise ingredient for a tossed salad. When I dumped in some leftover sauerkraut, the unexpected results excited my taste buds. I even shared the same theme on the air for a promotional piece with public TV, WSEC, but with a little different slant, of course. I discussed how sometimes events in our lives are surprising and unexpected but result in a marvelous experience.

For example, I am quite confident that both Abraham and Isaac were extremely surprised with the sudden change of events while on top of Mt. Moriah. Abraham was about to sacrifice his only son, following the directions of God. Son was placed on the altar, along with the wood. Son was a bit nervous, wondering if his father really planned on carrying through with this live offering—he, Isaac, being the living sacrifice. Father was undoubtedly wondering if he truly could carry out this action. And then, knife in hand, Abraham was about to draw blood when, surprise, surprise: The unexpected happened. The sauerkraut in their lives was heard bleating in the bushes. An unblemished ram took the place of Isaac. What a wonderful, but unexpected ending (Genesis 22:1–18).

Well, part II. Prior to sharing "Sauerkraut Part I" with friends, I jotted a note to my great-nephew telling him the theme: sauerkraut. I challenged him to think how in the world we might be able to use that topic as a lesson for the Lord. Would you believe it? That University of Alabama engineering student sent Auntie a second cabbage lesson. He took the time to go online and found a piece posted by Robert Berendt. This February 3, 2006, piece was entitled, "Sauerkraut—More than Cabbage" I admit that I had to smile a bit with pride with David's efforts. But on with the cabbage lesson.

Sauerkraut was developed as a way of preserving cabbage when refrigeration was unavailable. Through fermentation, the cabbage undergoes changes. Although it may be made in a variety of ways, the author Berendt shares his method. He takes a large crock, a cutting board, sharp knife, and the handle of one of his old hockey sticks. He cuts up the cabbage into narrow strips and fills the crock. Then he adds chopped garlic and onions, a bit at a time, while he is beating the daylights out of shredded cabbage with the hockey stick. The pickling spices and salt are added as he continues to beat this conglomeration until it begins to release some of the water content. This process breaks down the cells. When the crock is full of water, he places a plate on the top until some water actually floats over the top of the plate. Next, the rest of the job of fermenting—the change of cabbage to sauerkraut—is just beginning.

So what lessons can we take from this process? What changes do we as humans go through as the greatest sauerkraut maker of all takes over our lives?

I am reminded of the TV program "Extreme Makeover." The owners leave. A crew enters the home with a wrecking ball and creative geniuses. Within a short time, miracles happen. Family and friends hardly recognize the old place. So also with our new relationship with the Lord. When we give our life over to Christ and His Kingdom, we become a "new" person (2 Corinthians 5:17). We are born again. Figuratively speaking, using our cabbage analogy, we must be transformed into new sauerkraut. God helps us add seasoning: a bit of love, a dash of service to others, a jug of joy, plus other elements so that we are changed. "Put off your old self, which is being corrupted by its deceitful desire; to be made new in the attitude of your minds; and to put on the new self, created to be like God in true righteousness and holiness" (Ephesians 4:22b–24). And we thought the change in cabbage to sauerkraut was dramatic.

We are transformed. "And we, who with unveiled faces all reflect the Lord's glory, are being transformed into his likeness with ever-increasing glory, which comes from the Lord" (2 Corinthians 3:18). Transformed.

From controlled by Satan to controlled by God.

From sinner to saint. Yes, we will still sin, but we may request forgiveness of our Father.

From lost to found.

From dead to alive. (A real purpose in our lives to serve and glorify our God.)

From lonely to having a forever friend, Christ.

One quick taste, and diners know whether they are eating cabbage or sauerkraut. Similarly, folks around us must be able to swiftly identify us as one of His by our actions, words, and spirit. We are not beaten with a hockey stick to incur a changed life. Nevertheless, change is tough. Begin and continue the fermentation process (Romans 6:6).

Be brave. Be courageous. Become Christian sauerkraut.

Surrounded by Love

**Everyone needs love, support, and warmth
from caring family and friends.
Love, however, is not a one-way street. To receive, we must give.
That is the problem.**

OUR PENGUIN FRIENDS DEMON-STRATE this two-way relationship. When the weather is especially frigid, the adults gather all of the young into a tight group. Then the mamas and the papas surround the children, feather-to-feather, providing shelter and warmth for the offspring. They, too, just like you and me, are warm-blooded. They must keep warm to survive. Their blubber helps. In addition, they have layers of down feathers, which they rub with oil from glands to make them waterproof and windproof. This helps but is insufficient to protect from severe winter storms.

The Creator, therefore, provided our feathered friends with another form of protection: the "huddle instinct." When the weather is blustery, as many as five thousand penguins will cluster together—feather to feather—supporting the entire group. The young are placed in the center for double protection. Animal love cares, supports, and warms each other. Alone, none would survive. Praise the Lord for His perfect creation.

But what about His other warm-blooded creation? Are we any different? Can we stand alone, especially at the height of our personal storms? In times of sickness, death, depression, loneliness, joy, celebration, or other highs and lows in our lives, what do we crave? Human contact. Connection with others. Hugs. Listening ears. Love and warmth from friendship. We, too, must huddle around each other, but it takes two plus to create these connections of togetherness. We absolutely cannot be a Lone Ranger in life. We were made by God to fellowship, support, and care for one another.

The scriptures remind us of Moses during the battle between the Amalekites and the Israelites. While Joshua led the army in battle, Moses promised to hold up his arms. As long as his arms were extended, Joshua's team continued winning. Hands down—they faced destruction. A problem arose, however, as Moses got tired. His arms would drop in fatigue. Then the solution, a team approach. Aaron and Hur sat Moses down on a rock and each held up an arm in support of Moses until sunset. The result was victory for the Israelites and for God (Exodus 17:8–16).

Paul admonishes us to "carry each other's burdens and in this way you will fulfill the law of Christ" (Galatians 6:2).

The apostle John whispers a reminder: "My command is this: Love each other as I have loved you. Greater love has no one than this, that he lay down his life for his friends" (John 15:12–13).

In Hebrews, we hear the words, "Let us not give up meeting together, as some are in the habit of doing, but let us encourage one another—and all the more as you see the Day approaching" (Hebrews 10:25). I love the admonition to "encourage."

Paul expressed his appreciative of his fellow workers, Priscilla and Aquila, in his letter to the Romans: "They risked their lives for me. Not only I but all the churches of the Gentiles are grateful to them" (Romans 16:3b–4).

When believers join hands, we grow in faith. We become a model for Christ, demonstrating His love and forgiveness. Christians in the early church "continually devoted themselves to the apostles' teaching and to fellowship" (Acts 2:42). They taught one another and had fellowship. Fellowship and worship certainly are not limited to a church building, but isolation from other believers robs one of the care, concern, and support human beings need. You need other Christians, and they need you.

The *New York Post* headline announced, "Millennials Are Choosing Pizza, Push-Ups, and Video Games over Church." We who have white hair, weak knees, or weird wrinkles must wake up, reach out, and love these young folks. How are you personally caring and loving those especially turned off by organized religion? Take inventory. List two or three neighbors, friends, or crazy youth who might need comforting arms, listening ears, or an experienced example. Develop a community of friends and support each other.

Surround each other with love.

Our Minds

Battle for Control

Disaster! Distress! Emptiness!

IMAGINE YOURSELF IN THE ruins of an ancient, scholarly library. The ceiling is tumbling down on top of oaken tables. Books are scattered, torn, and waterlogged. Furniture is broken and discarded. And to top off the ruin, we find a trio of trees bursting through the neglected floor. Things are out of control. What was once a wonderful depositor of knowledge and excitement is useless. Rot instead of reading. Death for literacy of the mind.

The viewer is left to wonder what happened. Was it storm damage? Lack of money? War damage? Too many electronic devices so no one found books a source of wisdom? What caused the disaster? Where, today, are readers going for food for their minds? No books. No quiet retreat. All is lost.

What about our minds, the seat or library of our intellect? Are our thoughts filled with the rubble of fear and worry? Have we discarded moments of thoughtful review of the scriptures? Do we spend more time filling the brain with evil thoughts, jealousy, and doubt rather than with friendship, kindness, and joy? What is stored in your brain? Could it be recipes, anniversary dates, best fishing spots, or baseball scores? Has the memory forgotten or discarded familiar hymns of praise or scriptures learned as a child? Take a quick inventory of your mind. Are thoughts of hope and peace dust-covered and broken? Are your nights swamped with regret and discouragement? Do you seem to have nightly battles with the devil and wake up dragging and dull? Maybe your mind resembles our mental image of a library: dusty, broken, weary, and worn. Time for remodeling and renovation. Get out the dust rag. Fill the garbage can with your sadness and start afresh. Renew your mind with four familiar but sometimes forgotten actions.

1, 2, 3, ready, go.

Rejoice in the Lord always; again I will say, Rejoice. Let all men know your forbearance. The Lord is at hand. Have no anxiety about anything, but in everything by prayer and supplication with thanksgiving let your requests be made known to God. And the peace of God, which passes all understanding, will keep your hearts and your minds in Christ Jesus. Finally, brethren, whatever is true, whatever is honorable, whatever is just, whatever is pure, whatever is lovely, whatever is gracious, if there is any excellence, if there is anything worthy of praise, think about these things. What you have learned and received and heard and seen in me, do; and the God of peace will be with you. (Philippians 4:4–9 RSV)

Fill the shelves of your mind with

- **Praise and Rejoicing** for our salvation, beautiful world, loving family, and freedom to worship and to read and study His Word. Rejoice in spite of our many life challenges, for God is still in charge. Praise the Lord.
- **Patience.** Fill your minds and hearts with thanksgiving and praise, and there will be little room left for anxiety and fear. Wait on the Lord. He does not always move at the speed we desire, but He is faithful to the end. Wait, and again I say wait and be patient. (An almost impossible action for this writer.) Focus on others. Ignore slights. Praise God instead, and peace will follow.
- **Prayer.** The Lord is near, not just His return, but near you every moment. Open up those peepers and watch for His wondrous

works. He is a friend, helper, and source of wisdom. Talk daily with Him. Yes, just conversational talk—not fancy words. Plead for help in loving others. Pray expecting comfort. Develop a thankful heart. Do not let the devil control your mind. Post a guard around your heart by trusting God.

- **Purity.** We are to think about "whatever is pure, lovely, and gracious." Now that is tough these days, but if we fill the brain with thoughts, words, and actions that focus on God, we will shove out the dusty, broken, harmful clutter of the world. Create new brain shelves for storage of the love of God. Then invite pure thought clients to enter and enjoy.

Pray for restoration of your mind, including peace and joy.

Delilah's Ancestors Found

Ancient Philistine Cemetery Discovered
on the Southern Coast of Israel

ARCHAEOLOGISTS MAY HAVE FINALLY uncovered evidence of one of the ancient enemies of the Hebrew people: the Philistines. This cemetery outside the walls of ancient Ashkelon existed between the twelfth and seventh centuries BC.

Discovery of a cemetery containing more than two hundred individuals hopefully will provide information about the origin, life, and burial practices of this group of people. Prior to the discovery, understandings about the Philistines were "about as accurate as the mythology relating to George Washington chopping down the cherry tree," says Lawrence Stager, archaeologist at Harvard University.

According to the Hebrew Bible, these Philistines warred with the Israelites. This uncircumcised group was among the most notorious villains of the period. They controlled the modern-day region of southern Israel and the Gaza Strip. The powerful Philistines even seized the Ark of the Covenant for a time.

Among their people was the lovely lady Delilah. This devious female tangled with Sampson, chopped off his hair, and subjected him to hard labor in a Gaza prison. Later, as his hair returned, Sampson sought out the Lord and prayed for forgiveness (Judges 16). During a pagan sacrificial ritual, the Philistines gathered in Gaza to celebrate. Sampson, the prized prisoner, was brought into the temple to the shouting of jeering crowds. Sampson managed to brace himself between twin pillars and push the temple down, crushing all, including himself. What a guy.

The giant Goliath was also a Philistine. We remember Goliath when the shepherd lad David challenged this behemoth figure with a slingshot and five pebbles, bringing him crashing to his death.

Finding the Philistine cemetery was a fantastic event. There was evidence their homeland might be somewhere in the Aegean, but no human remains were found. The Leon Levy Expedition had been excavating Ashkelon since 1985. In 2013, they decided to dig some test pits outside of the city's north wall but came up with nothing. The final day of digging arrived. They had only thirty minutes left until the backhoe operator announced he would drive off.

And then it happened. Adam Aja, assistant curator at Harvard's Semitic Museum, found himself staring into an empty pit. Frustrated, he kept digging and hit what looked like bone fragments. He lowered himself into the pit in the bucket of the backhoe to investigate. What did he find? A human tooth. And so began the excavations of these early Canaanites.

For more details, go to news.nationalgeographic.com.

It's wonderful how once again scientific efforts support the information in our Bible.

Unheard Carols by a Little-Known Cast

THE AIRWAVES, MALLS, HOMES, and our heads ring with familiar melodies of the Christmas season. Santa Claus alternates with the Christ Child. We hum along with three French hens, angels on high, and sleighs dashing over the snow. "Silent Night" is sung more frequently than the National Anthem. This truly is a season of old favorites, and most of it relates to our Savior.

As I sit here writing, my mind shoots back in time. Perhaps if I listen very, very carefully, I will be able to hear the animals moving around in an ancient Bethlehem stable. Do I hear Joseph pacing in the straw as he waits for his stepson to arrive? Mary is weary with waiting but so trusting of the promise made to her nine months previously (Luke 1:28). She is to give birth to Jesus, the Son of the God. I wonder what this very young mother was thinking? Perhaps she nervously hummed a little lullaby.

Reviewing Luke 1 and 2, we discover at least four little tuneless melodies celebrating this miracle birth. No, the Bethlehem Philharmonic was not present. Decca had no contract for the record's release. CNN's tenacious reporters were nowhere to be found, but music was there.

Zachariah had a song of faith. An angel of the Lord appeared to him with the announcement that he and his wife were to have a son. Zachariah wondered aloud how in the world they were to have a son, since they were long past child-bearing years. Gabriel gave him a sign: "You will be silent until this promise is fulfilled." For nearly 270 days, Zach was speechless. And then, the miracle: the birth of a son. At the time of circumcision, the family announced that the babe would be called Zachariah, after his father. But oh, no. Daddy announced in writing that the child's name was John. Immediately, his mouth was opened, and he could praise God and speak once again. All were amazed and wondered, "What then is this child going to be?" (Luke 1:65). This faithful father spontaneously shared a message of mercy and proclaimed the mission of son John to prepare the way for the Lord's coming (Luke 1:67–80). What glorious news for the world that day.

A few months later, lonely sheepherders were startled by the message from a heavenly choir: a song of peace. "Glory to God in the highest heaven, and on earth peace to men on whom his favor rests" (Luke 2:14). Certainly on that night, these simple shepherds did not fully understand the significance of this message of peace, but they took action. Off they trotted, maybe staff in hand or lambs tucked under their arms, to visit the Christ Child.

About three months prior to the birth of John, another melody was heard. Mama Mary visited her cousin Elizabeth and shared a message through song. She began the libretto of trust and thanks with, "My soul glorifies the Lord and my spirit rejoices in God my Savior" (Luke 1:46–47). She voiced her praise of the Mighty One but also acknowledged the fact that she was but a humble servant. Hers was a song of trust that God was in control of her life.

And then, a song of hope. A devout follower, Simeon had only one item on his bucket list: to see the Promised One before he died. The Holy Spirit had revealed to him that he would live to see the Lord's Messiah. At the time of circumcision of Jesus, Simeon was present in the temple. He was even allowed to hold the child, and thus our fourth song: "Sovereign Lord, as you have promised, you may now dismiss your servant in peace. For my eyes have seen your salvation" (Luke 2:29). He waited all of his life, and then this wonderful reward: to be allowed to see the Lord, to proclaim His sovereignty, and to bless the child.

Faith, peace, trust, hope. Won't you join me today in singing a hymn of praise to our sovereign Lord?

Surviving the Fire down into the Water

TRAPPED. GRIPPED BY FEAR. The world on fire. Flames leaped closer to their home. Then they remembered their neighbors' pool.

> Penny told herself to calm down. Hyperventilating under water would be deadly.

Penny, and her husband, Hank, debate whether to immerse themselves in the swimming pool next door or run for their lives. Then suddenly, a giant tree next to the pool goes up in flames. The wooden railroad ties framing the concrete steps leading to the pool ignite. The heat becomes unbearable. Stripping off most of their clothing, Hank directs Penny to jump in now.

Holding T-shirts to protect their faces from the burning embers when they must surface for air, the couple leaps in. Penny is wearing a thin top and PJ bottoms. Her glasses have disappeared. They move away from many of the burning objects flying around. Fortunately, the pool is only four feet deep. They are freezing. To stay warm, they hold each other, but when they must surface to breathe, the air is intensely hot. The phone which she had placed in her shoe at the edge of the pool has melted from the heat.

For over six hours, the couple remained submerged. When they finally exited the water, their home, car, cocker spaniel, and all belongings were ash. "But we are alive," Hank murmurs as they hold hands and walk out.

Many similar survival stories emerged from the 2017–18 California wildfires. As I read about these numerous survival experiences, I immediately thought about the scriptures and fire and water. When the Lord was disappointed with the behavior of people in Sodom and Gomorrah, He rained down brimstone and fire and destroyed everything in the area—much like California. Only Lot and his two daughters were saved (Genesis 19:12–30). God can destroy.

Or remember when Moses observed an angel of the Lord in a blazing fire in the midst of a bush? Wonder of wonders, however, the bush was not consumed. God can do amazing things (Exodus 3:1–3). History tells us how Moses led the Children of Israel to safety through a giant pool, the Red Sea (Exodus 14:13–31). God can work miracles.

Noah, his family, and a menagerie of animals floated on water for forty days, survived the devastation of the world, and then returned to land, ready to replenish the world with new life (Genesis 7:1–8:22). God is good.

Penny and Hank would have appreciated the promise God spoke to Israel through the voice of Isaiah: "When you pass through the waters, I will be with you; and when you pass through the rivers, they will not sweep over you. When you walk through the fire, you will not be burned; the flames will not set you ablaze. For I am the Lord, your God, the Holy One of Israel, your Savior" (Isaiah 43:2–4). God can control the elements of fire and water for good. The New Living Translation of this same verse adds a contemporary promise: "When you go through deep waters, I will be with you. When you go through rivers of difficulty, you will not drown. When you walk through the fire of oppression, you will not be burned up; the flames will not consume you." God takes care of His children.

What marvelous promises. Have you ever walked through days of difficulty and stress or faced apparently unsolvable problems? Has grief gripped your mind and heart? Your life may have some burned areas and challenges, just like our pool divers, but in the end, the promise of God to be with you remains. Breathe deeply, submerge in a pool of His love, and then continue walking over the ashes and ruins of life, but with hope in your heart. Don't give up. Just as this couple must pick of the pieces of destruction and move forward, so must you, scars and all.

Then one final reference to water: as we admit our weakness, acknowledge God's grace and forgiveness, and are immersed into the waters of baptism, we die to sin and are born again and rise to walk as a Child of God.

> **God can save us. We can begin again. We walk
> with Him as He restores our souls.
> Go forward and begin a new life.**

A Christ-Centered Life: What Would That Be Like?

AS WE CONCLUDE THESE essays, let's take one final look at what it means to be a Christian, to be like Christ. Many lessons and sermons dwell on "How to …?" How to be kind, happy, family friendly, neighborly, or generous. When is the last time we seriously looked at the life of Jesus? He is our model for actions during times of pain, sorrow, joy, or loneliness. Have we become too self-centered rather than Christ-focused in our studies and lives?

If we are born again, Christ dwells in us, and the old person (me) is put aside. "To them God has chosen to make known among the Gentiles the glorious riches of this mystery, which is Christ in you, the hope of glory" (Colossians 1:27). We are to let His love, energy, habits, and decisions be our model. Are our lessons and sermons no different from what any moral person might follow? Perhaps we are spending an inordinate amount of time satisfying our personal needs and desires. Are we praying only for self, family, or friends' wants and needs versus Kingdom building with followers modeling His behaviors? Are our prayers similar to the following?

> "God help me get out of debt; help me carry my Bible to
> worship; help me listen to Christian music more."
> "Make me well. Take away this pain. And Lord,
> if you don't mind, do it quickly."
> "Stop the quarreling between my son and his wife."
> **"If it is okay with you, Lord, help me stop smoking
> [beating my husband, being grumpy]."**

> "Remind me, Lord, to have warm, fuzzy moments around
> the church coffeepot with fellow believers."

There is nothing wrong with those actions and prayers, but fellowship with Christ is much more. Jesus reached out to sinners and followers alike. His presence and teaching were not limited to a formal gathering of followers. He spoke out in the temple and at the seaside. He touched peoples' hearts while thousands gathered on a hill or a single person sat listening by the well. He went fishing and taught the guys in a boat. While attending a wedding reception, He even scolded His mom in a gentle fashion. He cried over the lost. Anger was demonstrated with the temple merchants. In other words, He was God's Son everywhere He went, all the time, with everyone. So what does that mean to you and me?

The Kingdom of heaven is not built with people just being good, hugging fellow believers, or following rules and regulations. The Kingdom is built on Jesus, the Crucified One. It includes alternative thinking and mind-sets. It must be a Christ-centered perspective.

"On that day you will realize that I am in my Father, and you are in me, and I am in you" (John 14:20).

Jesus must be central to our lives. He is a key figure and essential to our fellowship. He is the key to our joy.

How does that translate into action? God loved us so much that He gave His Son for us as the ultimate sacrifice. He gave His all to rescue us. We do not come under His blood through good deeds and a routine prayer life. I cannot earn my salvation through overcoming my faults. Salvation is a gift, freely given, but I must accept that gift. I cannot leave it wrapped up in a package under the tree. I must open my heart and life and let Christ enter. Then things change. I become a new person. My prayers and daily conversation will become, ideally, the words of Christ popping out of my mouth. Examples:

> "God, thank you for the life I have, but help it reflect Your love
> today. Remind me to think before I speak out in anger."
> "Lord, while visiting with my doctor [or cabinet builder or store
> clerk], may I in some way reflect my love and trust in You. May
> I witness positively versus grumbling and mumbling so that
> when I leave, each will know You were present in that visit."

"Yes, God, help me to not only enjoy a greasy, sweet donut
with fellow Christians, but help me reach out to someone
who is lonely, hurting, dirty, or broke and share conversation
and love, even in an uncomfortable setting."

Wow. That may be tough. But that is what reaching out to the whole world is about. He came to save all, not just the folks meeting at our worship center.

And then be full of joy. How? John wrote these things "to make our joy complete" (1 John 1:4):

God, help me not to be one of those religious people who sees little to smile about. Religion is serious, but as a Christian, help me smile. Remind me, Lord, that I have a wonderful promise of life with You. You have promised me security and peace. Help me to accept that peace. May others *not* think of me as Ms. Sourpuss.

Let joy flow from my life everywhere I go. Focus on Him always

Fun Challenge Quiz

YOU MAY BE CURIOUS about the author. Embedded throughout these essays is background information. How much do you remember? The educator in me has created a mini-quiz. There will be no grades given. Have fun and see what you now know about Kathryn Ransom. The number at the end of each question refers to the essay in which the answer may be found.

Good luck.

1. What is the location and date of birth of the author? #11

2. What keepsake did she receive on the day of her birth? #62

3. In what town does she currently live? #7

4. What was the name of her brother? #8

5. Recently she completed an important item on her bucket list. What was that accomplishment? #68

6. Who would she most like to be like, in addition to Christ? #66

7. During a repair job, she swallowed an unusual object. Name that object. #72

8. What well-known book did her father read aloud while she was young? #34

9. Who was her dad's employer for almost his entire working career? #66

10. What was one of the colleges she attended? #7

11. Although she needed help, what water adventure did she experience one time in Mexico? #43

12. What small item belonging to her mother still sits on her dresser? #82

13. When helping a new church prepare for worshippers, what "exciting" task was she assigned? #92

14. How might you describe her cooking skills, based on information in #13 and #94?

15. Annually, for a number of years, the author has visited a large city. Where was she and what little gem did she discover one Sunday? #30

16. Who provided the kernel of an idea for the second essay on sauerkraut? #95

17. The author has had the privilege of traveling a great deal. What two countries are mentioned in essay #42?

18. Based on comments in several essays, what fruit of the spirit would you think might be a challenge for the author? #54

19. Thought question: Based on these essays, how might you describe the author to a friend? You are on your own for this answer.

Thanks for taking a minute to get to know
Kathryn (Kathy, Katie, K.A.).
I hope that one day, we will meet some of you along our path.
If so, please say hi.

About the Author

KATHY IS AN EDUCATOR and Christian leader. She is actively involved in her community, including as a trustee for the Illinois Symphony Orchestra, the local public television station WSEC, and Lincoln Christian University. Traveling, golf, and classical music help identify this eighty-plus-year old author. "Life is an adventure," explains her enthusiasm for constantly searching for new challenges, e.g., writing her first book at the age of eighty-three.

Kathy graduated from Southwest Missouri State and the University of Illinois. Her entry into the world of education began in a fourth-grade inner-city classroom, followed five years later as a consultant for a major school publisher, and then the coordinator of the reading and English program for Springfield Public Schools. Following retirement, Ms. Ransom worked with teachers and school districts from the coast of California to Long Island, New York, as well as doing considerable adjunct teaching for several area colleges. During that time she also served on the board of the International Reading Association, including the role of president.

She is active with the area Christian service camp, a "worker bee" for a local group for senior adults (Academy of Lifelong Learners), and other community service groups. Life is a joy when busy and helping others remains a constant bottom line philosophy of her life.